Praise for Sea...

"Emma Kathryn has supplied a prof... and its correlation to the Wheel of the Year. In this book, Emma provides exercises that help a practitioner connect in concert with both the seasons of the year and the spirit of the land. From working with plants to the planets and their corresponding days of the week, there is a spiritual playlist of sorts in this approach to Animism, which undulates throughout. Not only has she reflected upon a practice that works with the larger cycles of the year, but also Emma takes into consideration the smaller cycles in nature as well, such as those of the sun and the moon. With explorations, exercises, visualizations, and meditations, this book will provide insight into expanding the practice of witches, both new to the path and seasoned alike." — **Vincent Higginbotham, author of *How Witchcraft Saved My Life* and *Thrifty Witchery***

"Emma Kathryn lovingly shows us how to navigate the cycles of contemporary life by honoring and working with the allies we meet along the way." — **The Magickal Women Conference**

"Emma Kathryn has done the intensive work of studying, learning, reassessing, and unlearning the teachings and practices of the Wheel of the Year to put into writing the core and heart of these traditional teachings from a practical, modern, and animistic perspective, inviting the reader (regardless of their religious traditions) to reassess their connection to nature and spirits. Making use of the days of the week, the lunar phases, and all kinds of active exercises, *Season Songs* invites you to reconnect with the essence of local spirits and deities, to discover the mysteries of the earth and its seasons, and to embrace those secrets that the spirits of nature have safeguarded for you." — **Elhoim Leafar, author of *Dream Witchery***

"Emma Kathryn takes the reader on a wonderful and enspirited journey that centers an animist practice while exploring the cycle of sabbats, seasons and one's life. Pulling in folklore and her own personal explorations, this book is a wonderful companion that could serve as an almanac and welcome accompaniment to one's practice."
—**Nathan M. Hall, author of** *Path of the Moonlit Hedge*

season
songs

About the Author

Emma Kathryn (Nottinghamshire, UK) is a staff writer at *Witch Way Magazine*, *The House of Twigs* blog, *Stone, Root, and Bone* blog, the *Spiral Nature* blog, and *Gods & Radicals*. She hosts *Wild Witch Podcast* and has spoken at several UK Pagan events, including Magickal Women Conference in London. Visit her online at www .EmmaKathrynWildWitchcraft.com.

Season songs

Rediscovering the Magic in the Cycles of Nature

emma kathryn

Llewellyn Publications
Woodbury, Minnesota

FIRST EDITION
First Printing, 2023

Book design by Christine Ha
Cover art by Sylvie Demers
Interior illustrations by the Llewellyn Art Department

Llewellyn Publications is a registered trademark of Llewellyn Worldwide Ltd.

Library of Congress Cataloging-in-Publication Data (Pending)
ISBN: 978-0-7387-7117-5

Llewellyn Worldwide Ltd. does not participate in, endorse, or have any authority or responsibility concerning private business transactions between our authors and the public.

All mail addressed to the author is forwarded but the publisher cannot, unless specifically instructed by the author, give out an address or phone number.

Any internet references contained in this work are current at publication time, but the publisher cannot guarantee that a specific location will continue to be maintained. Please refer to the publisher's website for links to authors' websites and other sources.

Llewellyn Publications
A Division of Llewellyn Worldwide Ltd.
2143 Wooddale Drive
Woodbury, MN 55125-2989
www.llewellyn.com

Printed in the United States of America

Other Books by Emma Kathryn

Wild Witchcraft
Witch Life

Contents

◆◆◆◆◆◆

Exercises

◆◆◆◆◆◆

Introduction

◆◆◆◆◆◆

The world is an amazing place, wouldn't you agree? So full of mystery, even today in this scientific age. With all our technology, the world still holds many secrets—truths that can be felt and sensed rather than measured and quantified. Even if we just consider ourselves and our very existence—that we are the product of thousands of people coming together in love—it's pretty mind blowing. For many witches, occultists, and those interested in the esoteric, working with the spirits of those who came before, the ancestors, is an important part of their practice. There are many books, essays, podcasts, and videos that deal with the topic of ancestor worship and veneration, hinting at its popularity. And it makes sense doesn't it, to honour those who came before? They are family, after all.

And yet, spirit work, of which ancestor worship is just one thread, is a wide and varied tapestry with many different beliefs and practices.

Many people are coming to realise that the world around them is also imbued with spirit. Perhaps you have always felt there is more to this world than what can be seen—that there is a depth to seemingly simple things. For example, a flower is not just a flower but is instead a part of the environment to which it owes its existence. It is the pollen carried on the wind or the tiny hairs of a bee; it is the bee itself, the hive. It is the seed from the parent plant and the parent plant itself. It is the sun and the rain, the soil; it is everything.

It is spirit too.

I know I have always felt there is a deeper level of being beyond the physical world, one that is connected to it and to us. The outdoors and nature have always been a soul soother, and for many years, I didn't realise what I felt, what I *knew*, had a name. I didn't know others felt this way too. And so when I stumbled upon animism as a belief, as a way of living in this world, a way of being, I was overjoyed. Others felt and saw the same interconnectedness to the world around them that I, too, felt. It was a great feeling, that initial discovery, and it seemed to confirm my own beliefs and ideas. But after the initial excitement that comes with any meaningful discovery, particularly of the self, I was left with some soul searching to do.

You see, this discovery of animism as a distinct concept then led me to really consider how I lived my everyday life and to examine my spiritual and magical practices. Animism was the thread that ran through each seemingly separate part of my life. It was what connected my distinct and individual magical practices, which include British Traditional Witchcraft, Obeah, and Vodoun. And while it didn't necessarily change how I practised each of them, it did make me consider things on a deeper level in a way I hadn't before. It is this that has truly empowered the magical, spiritual, and mundane areas of my life and continues to do so.

And so, my fellow seekers, I find myself here writing this small book for those who, like I do, feel the interconnectedness of all things, who find solace in the land and seek a deeper relationship with the spirits that reside there in the trees, the mountains, the rivers and oceans; for those who hear the many and varied voices of nature within the very land where we live, no matter where that is.

In writing this book, it is my hope that we can begin an animist revolution in which we come to see the world not as something separate from ourselves but as it truly is: alive with spirit. By doing so, we come to recognise our own place and space within the world and realise that we are not just separate entities but connected to the land, the spirits, and one another. Let us dance and sway to the songs of the land.

How to Use This Book

Within these pages some of my own stories are shared for the first time, stories that tell of my own awakening. In sharing these stories, I want to show you that animism is something that is common, a shared experience, one that though forgotten can be recaptured, the links restored.

You will discover stories from the land: personal and shared, folk stories, and lore. By sharing these, it is my hope that you will come to view the cycles of the land, seasons, and Wheel of the Year as alive and meaningful—old traditions that can add new meaning and depth to your own witchcraft practice today.

There are also a range of exercises for you to take part in. After all, the seasons and sabbats are real, tangible events that require action. For too long we have viewed the Wheel of the Year as the passive movement of time, something to be reminded of by a calendar. The exercises in this book will help you to navigate the land where you live in a meaningful way, creating embodied relationships that are founded on and shaped by your own experiences and interactions with that land. Among these exercises, you'll also find several guided visualisations and meditations. You might find it easier to make a recording of them and use this when doing them rather than reading them through and trying to remember the details.

The poems you'll find at the end of most chapters are some of my own experiences and feelings, mulled over, forgotten, remembered, and experienced again. These snapshots are the distilled essence of the seasons through my experiences with them and what they mean for me. They represent the accumulation of my journey at the point at which I wrote them. No doubt as I pass by again, as I continue on this spiral path, more experiences with the land and with spirit will be added to the lessons already learnt. These are the songs of my spirit, infused and enriched by the seasons and the cycles of nature, by the songs of the very land itself.

With this in mind, many of the exercises are designed to be done more than once. Sometimes you will be asked to go outside for a walk or to sit or stand. Sometimes this will be to observe certain times or occurrences, and other times it will be simply to immerse yourself in the landscape and to really feel and appreciate the different energies that abound at those times.

The activities are all designed to be active, even when they ask you to sit and watch or listen.

The Sabbats

All the seasons have two sabbats. As you work your way through this book, you'll see that instead of being a single day marked on the calendar, each sabbat marks a moment in the shifting of energies in which the genii locorum (singular, genius loci)—the indwelling spirits of a place, including flora and fauna—may be more keenly felt. By incorporating an animistic outlook—by recognising the spirit latent in all natural, living things and recognising the changes that occur throughout the seasons, both within the land and the spirits that reside there—we can make the sabbats and thus the Wheel of the Year relevant for today and our lives.

While exploring the cycles of the year in connection to the land where we live, we will recall the words and melodies to the songs of the seasons and begin to recall and rebuild our relationships with the spirits that reside within the land, creating new rhythms, tunes, and songs that will carry our connection to the land and the genii locorum into the future.

In my previous book, *Witch Life: A Practical Guide to Making Every Day Magical*, I gave lots of tools, recipes, spells, rituals, and more, all with the aim to inspire would-be witches and those more magically seasoned to get down and dirty with the practical aspects of magic and witchcraft. This book, then, is a follow-on of sorts.

Let me explain: I am a nerd by heart. I truly mean that. I love studying. If I'm interested in a topic, I want to read up on it as widely as possible. I love it. That is all well and good, but sometimes it is just too easy to stay there, comfortably distanced from the practical side of things. *Witch Life* was a witch's boot up the bum, inspired from my own much-needed kick up the arse in the first lockdown of Covid. It was time to get things done.

Now that some of those things are done and experience and firsthand knowledge have been gained, it's time to come back once more to digest and mull over, to discover new depths and meaning.

This is my hope with *Season Songs*. This book is about taking stock of your lived experiences and using them to infuse your own witchcraft and Pagan practice. This book transcends the artificial boundaries that mark so much of our everyday lives. It doesn't matter who you are, your tradition, who you love, or where you live. It cares not for skin colour or country. It cares only about rewilding our crafts and making them relevant in the land where each of us finds ourselves in this very moment and all the others that may come.

The season songs are our soundtrack to this wondrous beauty that is life. They inspire us, and this too is a form of spirit—the spirit of inspiration! Okay, perhaps that isn't what comes to mind when thinking about animism and the Wheel of the Year, but it is important to consider.

Let us not forget that we, too, are spirit and as such are a part of the land and nature. Our own voices add to the songs of the seasons of which we are all a part.

Chapter 1

The Wheel of the Year and the Cycles of the Seasons

◆◆◆◆◆◆

The Wheel of the Year is something of a modern invention, having become popular around the 1960s. It gives us as witches and Pagans a way of reconnecting with the cycles of the year. As a concept, it offers a view of the seasons not as simply the passing of time, but instead as a cyclical journey in which all beings play a vital and necessary part. The seasons are not something that just happens to the natural world; rather, it is the very world shifting, encompassing the hermetic principle of vibration. Everything is in flux; everything is constantly in motion. The seasons, then, within the framework of the Wheel of the Year are nature in motion. They are the constant ebb and flow of energies that are necessary for life itself.

It might make sense, then, that the Wheel of the Year and the seasons are linked to the agricultural year. For humans, settling into communities and farming as opposed to the hunter-gatherer, nomadic lifestyle marked a change for us and is perhaps the biggest defining factor of the species. Our lives today would no doubt be very different if ancient humans hadn't seen the benefits of forming settlements and farming animals and crops. If the seasons are the culmination of the flux of energies in an ever-turning cycle, then perhaps we can see these same energies govern farming: when crops are planted and harvested, when cattle should be bred and then slaughtered. Working with those energies, with the rise and fall of the seasons, allows for the successful growth and harvest of crops and animals.

Sounds awfully romantic, doesn't it?

And yet, many modern-day witches and occultists find themselves somewhat divorced from the concept of the Wheel of the Year.

Figure 1: Wheel of the Year

Perhaps one such reason is the fact that the wheel is very much based on the British and European agricultural year. If you live in a place where the seasons look so very different, why would the Wheel of the Year and the sabbats make any sense to your own experiences? And all of this is without even considering our modern lifestyles. While we are and always will be reliant on the combined efforts of nature and farming for our food and thus survival, so many people live lives out of sync with the natural rhythms. We work all year

round, artificially light and heat our homes, and can have food whenever we want, no matter the season, no matter where it's grown. In
so many ways, our ancestors were beholden to the natural cycles in a
way we no longer are, and this loss of connection might also explain
why the Wheel of the Year can be something of a turn-off, holding
little meaning beside offering token gestures for distant agricultural
events and customs that cannot be experienced firsthand.

For some, it might feel as though the spokes are coming loose,
the wheel buckled, so that it has become out of touch with the way
we live our lives today. It needn't be so.

By reconnecting with the land where we live and the natural
rhythms and cycles that occur there, we can more readily relate the
Wheel of the Year to our own lived experiences.

What Is Animism?

Animism can be described as the belief that everything has a spirit or
soul. Like most things in life, how far you take that belief depends on
you, and indeed varies from one practitioner to another. Some people
may believe literally everything in existence has a soul or spirit of sorts,
including everyday items or objects. Think about the energy and vibration of each thing, the processes that have shaped and forged it. In this
way, those items might acquire an aura or energy, a spirit. Other people may differ slightly and only hold that items found in nature have a
soul, and of course, there's room for everything in between!

Regardless of variation within the definition, generally, we can
see that animism is a belief that every natural thing has a spirit or
soul, and what's more, each is connected. This sense of every living
thing being connected by some life source, energy, spirit, or whatever
you wish to call it also has a name: *anima mundi*. This is my own
personal belief, that the natural world and everything within it has a

spirit, is alive with spirit and that we are all connected to this, a part of it.

This concept might take on more meaning if you consider the other animals we share this world with. Anyone who has ever shared their life with a beloved pet will tell you that all you need to do is look into their eyes to know they have a soul, a spirit. We can also see that whether one believes in a creator god or not, the fact is that the world just seems to, well, *work*. All the seemingly different aspects each contribute in a meaningful and necessary way to what we call life. When we consider these definitions of animism, as much as they make sense, they do little to truly capture the spirit (no pun intended) of what animism truly means. Indeed, the only way we can begin to truly understand animism is to experience it for ourselves.

I grew up and still live in a small rural town in the middle of England, UK. The housing estate my family lived on was in a poor area of town, a council estate, or for those in other parts of the world, social housing.

There were four of us kids altogether, myself and my three sisters. My parents always worked. My mum was a barmaid and cleaner, my dad a scrap man, and they both worked long hours.

One of my most meaningful encounters with spirit, with animism, occurred when I was around seven or eight years old. I was off school ill. Not the kind of ill that requires bedrest, mind, but ill enough to warrant a day off school nonetheless. And I was bored. There was no internet back then, no streaming sites, no children's twenty-four-hour TV channels.

Sensing my boredom, my mum suggested we take the dogs out, and not to any of our usual haunts either, but to the woods instead. I jumped at the chance, and I think that part of the excitement was just getting to spend some one-on-one time with my mum, a rare treat indeed! And so we got suited and booted before piling into the car with the dogs, and off we went.

I remember it was autumn. People always talk about those beautifully sunny and still-warm autumn days. My favourite, though, are those autumnal days when the skies are blanketed in grey clouds, heavy with the promise of rain; those days when a cool wind carries the scent of nature, sweetly spiced with the onset of decay and you can feel the dampness in the air. This was one such day. The trees were at their most glorious, ablaze with oranges, yellows, and reds. My illness was soon forgotten as we weaved our way into the woods, the dogs running free, simply enjoying the fresh air in their faces and the loamy forest floor beneath their feet. I remember stopping every so often, exploring this and that or plucking some treasure off the ground, a pinecone or acorn perhaps.

As unexpected as going to the woods had been—and indeed it was a real treat—it was still a normal ramble through the woods. Nothing extraordinary or special.

Or so I thought.

The track we were following was wide, one of the main pathways through the woods and a common trail for dog walkers, and yet I don't remember seeing anyone else. My mum was walking in front while I trailed behind, and the dogs were every which way between. I must have gotten sidetracked by something or other I'd found on the ground because when I looked up, I couldn't see my mum, though I could hear the dogs in the undergrowth. I wasn't panicked or scared and knew my mum was just around the curve in the path, but I was still just a little kid in the woods, and so I picked up my pace.

As I rounded the bend, I stopped.

It was like I had walked into one of my favourite books. The woods, transformed, were no longer an ordinary place in the ordinary world but were instead a magical land, the forest of Mrs. Tiggy-Winkle and Squirrel Nutkin, perhaps—characters from my favourite childhood author, Beatrix Potter.

Golden leaves caught in the breeze and floated down to the ground. Unseen, a stream swollen by the autumn rains gurgled and bubbled. The treetops swayed in the breeze, adding their own music to that of the stream and the birdsong too. In this place, time lost all meaning, and even now as I look back with my logical, adult mind, I couldn't tell you how long I stood transfixed. It was as though I had awakened from a grey dreamscape into a world alive.

In that moment, I knew this wood was alive in more than just the way we are taught. I could *feel* the life of this place, its spirit. I didn't know what this feeling was called, this sensing of a life force, of a spirit not only within the trees and birds but in everything, the very air itself. Yes, everything was individual, but they were connected too, and for the first time, I could sense these connections.

I have no idea how long we stayed in this part of the woods for, but I do know it was long enough for me to sit down, my back against a massive oak, feeling the rough bark and the steadfastness of it, delighting in the shower of leaves that danced down to the ground with every breath of wind. It felt like hours but in reality was prob-ably five minutes, ten at most. But regardless of how long we spent there that day, that moment has stayed with me. I see it as an import-ant spiritual marker. It was the first time I felt really connected to a place and was *aware* of that connection. It was the first time I *knew* a place was alive with something more than I could understand or put into words. Of course, now I know that what I am describing is animism, but to my childhood self, it felt like pure magic.

After that moment of awakening, as we continued on our walk through the woods, everything seemed more vibrant, more real. More alive. It didn't matter that we got a little lost, that by the time we'd made it back to the farmer's field where my mum had parked the car, we were on the wrong side. It didn't matter that we had to cross the muddy field in heavy rain. The cold rain felt delicious; the earthy scent that rose up from the ground was glorious. Nothing could dull or lessen the experience.

Nothing had changed and yet everything had changed.

I had changed.

The specifics will be different for sure, but that moment of discovery, that instant where you feel the interconnectedness of everything, when you recognise the spirit within yourself and the land around you, I think most people have encountered something similar. Which then begs the question, why aren't more people animist?

I believe many people experience these things when they are children. Children, generally speaking, often have a sense of wonder about the world and all of the things in it. I have one niece who cares so much about animals that when we visit my gran, she spends most of the visit stroking and kissing the dog ornaments, and another of my nieces adopts pieces of fruit as pets! Cute childhood affections, for sure, but I also think these hint at the connection they feel between themselves and the other beings we share this world with.

Cast your mind back to your own experiences. Perhaps you felt a deep connection to a particular place, tree, or animal. No doubt some of the childhood instances and occurrences felt like pure magic at the time, whether that was playing in the woods, swimming in lakes, days out in nature, or even a garden. I just think we minimise these things as we get older. We grow up and lose something, that sense of wonder in the ordinary.

As I cast my mind back, there are so many moments, most of them so small as to be easily overlooked. Once, when I was in primary school, perhaps eight or nine, certainly no older, my teacher organised a teddy bears' picnic—not at school, mind, but in her own garden at home. I was so excited. For me, with my child's mind, teachers were these special creatures, seemingly all-knowing. Who knew they didn't live at school, that they were full people with full lives outside of the classroom?

And what a day it was! It was one of those afternoons, where the air is warm and thick like honey straight from the hive. At such moments, time itself loses all meaning—gossamer thin in some places, shimmering like the threads of a spider's web, while in others pooling deeply, dark depths that seem to hold the memory of the earth itself.

Stepping into that garden was like walking into the pages of *The Secret Garden*. Flowers dazzled in all colours, and bumblebees droned among the tall spikes of hollyhocks and foxglove in their shades of pink, yellow, purple, and white. And there among this oasis of colour in the hot afternoon was the pond, an old-fashioned claw-foot bathtub, and small, white water lilies flowered on the surface.

It was such a beautiful garden, and though it wasn't a wild space like the woods, the connection and recognition of spirit were the same.

Children, in my professional opinion as a teacher, have a deeper trust in their feelings and emotions than adults. Perhaps this is because they are still learning about the world, are still in that stage of processing where they rely so much on their sensory input. Perhaps it is also due to an innocent lack of inhibition, meaning they act in a way that is more natural, yet to be moulded by the responsibility that comes with growing up and an increasing awareness of and exposure to societal norms, who knows. As we grow up and go through school, our teens, and then on to work and adulthood, we become more reliant on logic and develop an understanding of the cultural norms and how they apply to ourselves. It is this process that can lead us to ignore and perhaps even forget our connection to the land and the spirits that reside there.

But people are beginning to remember.

Rewilding Our Spirits

I have many people ask me about spirituality and what it is I believe, and whenever we get around to the topic of animism, once I've explained what it means to me and what it might involve, people then often make parallels to their own beliefs, experiences, and actions.

When it comes to my own witchcraft practice and the individual practises routines, and beliefs it's composed of, animism stands at the core of each. It is the interconnecting thread that weaves them all together. It has deepened my craft in so many varied and nuanced ways by connecting it firmly to the land. In recent Pagan discourse, connection to land can often be a contentious issue when we consider colonialism and the far right, but in terms of your own individual and personal practice, you can only connect to the land where you are, wherever that may be and no matter how you got there. I write this from my own perspective, from my own familial and ancestral history, which does, in fact, include slavery and colonialism. Connecting to the land does, of course, include learning about the events that occurred there and being respectful to all the other beings within that space, people included.

Developing Connection

There will be various exercises throughout this book, each designed to help connect you to the seasons of the year, which will ultimately deepen your connection to the land and the spirits that reside there. I advise keeping a notebook or journal anytime, but particularly when starting something new. Writing down your thoughts and experiences is vital because no matter how much you might feel confident that you will remember everything, I can almost guarantee you will forget something, no matter how important and insightful it seems at the time. Writing about your experiences will also give you the time and space to really reflect on and explore them more deeply than you might otherwise.

On this foray into animism and how it connects with the Wheel of the Year, it is important to be honest with yourself. If you have an experience that isn't positive or not what you expected in a disappointing way, it's important to acknowledge these feelings so you can begin to work through them and gain a deeper understanding of yourself and why the experience impacted you as it did. These are all valid concerns, and one of the beautiful things about building a relationship with the land is recognising and acknowledging our own experiences without judgment and fear.

Exploration: Looking Back

The human mind is a complex thing, and things once thought forgotten can be unearthed with only a little digging. It should come as no surprise then that this exercise is all about remembering, about looking back and recalling.

You will need to set some time aside for this exercise, at least thirty minutes. Turn off the TV, put your phone on silent, sit in a comfy chair, and relax. It might be useful to play some relaxing music and have your notebook close by.

Let your mind drift over your memories. Think about those times when you've been in nature or with an animal. Allow yourself to recall those memories, to relive them. You'll find that once you begin, your mind finds its own track through your memory palace, but if you are having a little trouble getting started, a look through old photographs can help. You might initially believe you've never had any experiences with the land, nature, or spirit, but chances are you did. You might not recall them as eureka moments, so it's important you consider times and memories you might feel are just ordinary.

When you feel ready, choose two or three of those memories and write about them in your journal. As well as writing out a narrative of the event, try and include how you felt at the time as well as what you feel and think about the situation, event, or context now. Consider why that memory has stayed with you, the significance of it but also what happened next. Did it inspire a change within you? Did it set off a chain of reactions that led to some action or realisation?

You can repeat this exercise as often as you want, and you might find that sometimes you recall the same event, and this is perfectly fine. I often find that when an event or situation is meaningful, even if I don't understand why, I often circle back around to it. Sometimes there is no resolution, and yet other times, after what might feel like the hundredth time, all of a sudden there is some flash or recognition. This exploration is so important. As you explore your experiences, you will also uncover other truths and thoughts connected with them, and so this new insight might lead to a deeper understanding not only of yourself but also of the land and your connection to it.

Chapter 2
Meeting the Land

◆◆◆◆◆◆

I live in a rural town. I'm lucky that if I were to walk for ten minutes in any direction from my home, I would find myself in the woods, by the river, or in a field somewhere. That's without even considering those urban green spaces like parks and gardens. But, as rural as my town is, it is still an urban centre, where you'll find your big-name coffee shops, town centre chain stores, traffic, sprawling housing estates, and everything else you might expect with living in a town. If you live in a city, then the urban sprawl is even larger.

This can skew the image of the land where we live. The wild wood has become almost romanticised in modern culture, perhaps because we are so aware of climate change and pollution and how they affect those wild spaces. Not only that, even in small towns such as my own, we can see that those green spaces are pushed and squeezed, continually built on until those wild spaces become smaller and smaller until they cease to exist at all. All of this can lead to feelings of disconnect from the land where you live, which in turn leads to a disconnect with the spirits of the land. Eventually, this can affect your own connection with the cycle of the seasons and the very land itself.

In order to build that strong relationship with the land, you will need to meet the land, maybe for the first time. Or perhaps you require more of a reintroduction, a reacquainting, so to speak. This act in itself is the very first step in building that relationship with the land where you live and the spirits that reside there.

This getting to know the land occurs in many ways and reflects the multifaceted nature not only of the land but of ourselves. It is important to remember that this relationship is reciprocal, and much like the other relationships you have in your life, this one, too, takes effort. It is a relationship that is built in layers (or spirals, if you like), and as you move through this book and the cycles of the seasons, you will assimilate and build on your experiences so that each moment and occurrence informs the next and infuses new meaning and understanding.

Plant Communication

As you move through the cycle of the seasons and begin to tune in to their songs and melodies, you will come into close contact with plants and trees, and you will begin to communicate with them and they with you too. It is an inevitable part of the process.

Communicating with plants may sound airy-fairy, full-on woo (for the record, I love the woo too!), but you have been doing it your whole life!

Communication can mean many different things. My work with children and young people with autism has shown me firsthand just how diverse communication can be, from speech and signs to the things left unsaid. Communication is behaviours and reactions. It is relating to the world around you using all your senses while also sending out those very same vibrations and sensations yourself.

The scent of a flower carried on a gentle breeze is communication. The wind through the boughs is communication. The way a plant shows what it needs is communication: the way it stretches towards the light or how its leaves droop when in need of a shower. All of these methods of communication you are already familiar with; you just perhaps didn't think of them as communication. These are all very material, mundane methods of communication, and look how easy they are to overlook. No wonder, then, that the more subtle forms of communication are lost in the routine of the everyday.

As you begin to work more closely with the land where you live, it is only a natural part of the process that you will develop your senses and that these developed senses will more easily allow for communication between yourself and the other beings you share that space with.

It can be helpful to begin this process by looking after plants in your home and garden. Understanding the basic needs of plants and how they communicate those needs will give a good springboard from which to explore the wilder areas of your community.

Using plants in your witchcraft practice is also a good way of communicating with the spirit of that plant. The whole process is a spiral one—a cycle where with each revolution, the bond between witch and spirit is strengthened. Perhaps you'll start with growing herbs in your garden, which then extends to working with those plants in your practice, which in turn requires understanding how to process that particular plant. The more you understand that plant not only in terms of what it needs to grow and flourish, but also how to take from that plant while causing minimal harm, the more of the essence and spirit will carry over into your magical workings. This then feeds into developing and growing your relationship with the genius loci. It is not a one-sided relationship but is instead one based on mutual respect and understanding. As with all things, there is a give and a take, an ebb and a flow.

Have you ever been in a space, whether inside or out, and got a sense of feeling almost straight away? Perhaps it was an uncomfortable feeling that made you want to leave. Maybe you just felt calm and relaxed in that space for no logical reason. These can be sensations picked up from the genius loci.

I can remember taking the dogs to the woods one time, but instead of going to my usual patch, I decided we'd explore another part of the woods I'd never been to. As usual, we left the main path and took a shadier, wilder track beneath the boughs. At first, all was well. The dogs were loving life, chasing one another here and there, following whatever scent took their fancy, and I was feeling relaxed and at ease. After a while though, and I can't exactly pinpoint the moment, the realisation crept up on me that the dogs weren't following. My big Staffie, Boo, was waiting some metres back, and no amount of cajoling could make her take another step. It wasn't anything spooky, and the woods were quite safe. Yet there was a feeling of not quite being wanted there, or at least wherever I was heading to. And so I turned back and explored another part. Weird, huh?

In the time since then, sometimes I find my mind turning back to that memory and digging it back out as though time and distance might yield some understanding. Though I can't be certain, the more I think about this moment, the more it highlights an important aspect of respecting the land: sometimes we are not always wanted in a space.

When I go to the woods with friends who like to chatter and laugh on the way round (and there is nothing wrong with that), they often complain they don't see as many wild creatures as they thought they would. And of course, the simple and most obvious reason is that the creatures and spirits are cautious. Loud noises will startle and scare. Disrespect such as littering can damage and destroy. The collective harms of humanity against the natural world must be addressed, if only acknowledged. I happen to know that if you walk through that very same patch of woods quietly without strong perfume, listening and observing, you will be rewarded with glimpses of those wild beings that reside in such places.

Going into those spaces, listening to the land, and acting accordingly is a good way of laying those foundations that will ultimately lead to a strong relationship with that place.

It's worth pointing out that since then I have visited that part of the woods several times. But no matter how many times I go and am welcomed there, I am certain those initial feelings were indeed messages of a sort from the genius loci.

Plants on Your Altar

I often think that plant spirits can be some of the most difficult to begin to work with in a magical sense. When we work with the ancestors, it's easier because they were once human too. Even if they are ancestors you didn't know in life, they still understand the motivations and desires as well as the pains that come with living, and they have the same methods of communicating. You know that if someone is talking to you they want to tell you something, even if you don't understand the words. Your own human experience allows for an understanding that transcends language.

When it comes to communicating with plants, then, there are already barriers to overcome. One way of doing this is by keeping plants on your altar.

An altar is a sacred space, one where you can do your spiritual and magical work, and so this already sets the space aside from the other spaces in your home. If you don't have an altar, then you can set one up easily enough for this purpose, and the type of plant you have will ultimately determine where you might choose to locate it. All you really need in this space is a candle and your plant. If you have other meaningful items or tools, then you can include those as well.

Keeping a plant in this sacred space, a place where you go to practice your witchcraft, makes the plant an active participant in your craft. As you take care of your altar and your other tools, so too will you take care of the needs of the plant. I'll bet that before long you'll be talking to the plant, and in no time at all you'll have a feel for the plant and sense what it needs or when it needs some extra care and attention. This in turn will deepen your connection with it, which in turn will aid in plant communication.

As this relationship matures and grows, it will spread to the other plants you share your space with. In my own practice, I have found that this soon widens to include those plants and trees in my local landscape, though on a much larger scale!

Making the effort to be present, mindful, and active in this care of and communication with a single plant is something anyone can do and is a powerful and potent activity that can add so much to your own witchcraft practice as well as building the foundations of communicating with the land where you live.

Practical Making with Plants

Can you remember hot, stuffy days in classrooms? I can. And I liked school! But sometimes, especially if one's teacher was the uninspiring kind, then you might have found yourself watching dust motes swirl lazily on shafts of light, lost in daydreams of other worlds with grass beneath your feet and the sky overhead.

You should never just learn from books. Of course books are amazing things, but the best learning experiences come from doing the thing we want to do, whatever that is, when we get our hands dirty with experience. With this in mind, I believe working with plants even as a beginner is a great way of learning about that plant and developing your communication skills with nonhuman beings.

It breathes life into the words printed on pages, and when used in conjunction with them, can lead to a wonderful world of discovery and understanding.

Crafting Incense

Making your own incense is one of the easiest ways of getting practical with plants in a spiritual and magical sense. As much as this book is about rewilding the Wheel of the Year and making it more relevant to the cycles of the seasons and how they present where you live, it's also about changing your own perspectives. This is one of those "as above, so below" moments, when we build on our own understanding and experiences, shifting our perspective to gain a better understanding of the whole.

On the face of it, incense is an everyday item for many witches, a common tool of the trade you can pick up easily and cheaply. Why bother making your own? But consider the potency of an incense blended to work specifically with the spirits of a particular plant or place, one you know well. When you burn that incense, the smoke— the very element of air itself with its associations of movement and communication—becomes something else. It ceases to be simply smoke and instead transforms into a thread that connects you to that space, to the feelings, thoughts, and emotions you feel when you are in that place. It becomes a method in itself of communication with the spirits of that place and can help to bring them into a different space when doing ritual. This means that when working with a plant that is not local to you or grown by yourself, you can still bring the spirit of that plant into your ritual space with the use of incense.

When it comes to making your own incense, foraging items from a special or particular place is great if you can. If you can grow them, fantastic! But if you can't? Using herbs from the kitchen or essential oils is a good way of working with the spirits of a place or plant and makes a good alternative or substitution. As always, one should take care when buying ingredients, making sure—as far as is possible— they are ethically sourced and harvested. If you can use plant material you have grown yourself, then this is the best way of making sure they meet your ethical and moral standards. Growing your own also allows you to build a relationship with that plant, and this can also add to the depth of meaning and potency of your incense.

You have your dry ingredients, what now? Well, why not experiment? Use small amounts so that if a mix doesn't work, you don't waste too much. A good way to start is burning plant matter without mixing it. This will allow you to get a feel for each of the plants you are working with, whether their scent is strong or delicate. Next, try burning a mixture using equal amounts. Does it work well together? If not, how will you proceed? Will you add more of one and take some of the other? Or maybe something else is needed to balance the energies of the plants you are using? This method of fine-tuning will allow you to work in balance with different plants and will build up that familiarity of spirit.

Plants as Offerings

As with most areas of life and witchcraft, the seemingly separate aspects of spirit work are not as neat as we might like, nor should they be. In fact, the boundaries between those different, distinct aspects are not rigid, and each bleeds into the next.

Working with the spirits of plants can also form part of your ancestor worship or veneration. This bleeding and blending of what you may have previously considered to be different and separate aspects of spirit work can lend an intimacy to both, infusing each with that personal knowledge and experience that makes your relationship with that plant so totally unique and different from the next witch's relationship with it.

Fresh and dried plants, herbs, and flowers can be used as offerings within your practice. A good way of using them is in conjunction with your ancestors. By giving plants and flowers as offerings, perhaps a beloved's favourite bloom, then you can build on that connection. This is a good way to build on your altar work or to start a practice of sitting at an altar dedicated to working with spirit.

Having that familiar ancestral connection with spirit can help bridge the divide that working with plant spirits can sometimes cause.

Chapter 3
Lessons from the Past

◆◆◆◆◆◆

I adore folklore and everything it includes, such as folk magic, stories, and songs. There is something so utterly fascinating about folklore as a collective, made up of countless unique threads that can be woven together to hold the knowledge of a culture. But as interesting as folklore is, what does it have to do with magic, witchcraft, animism, and the cycle of the seasons?

First, the term *folk* tells us that these stories belong to the people of a culture. So often, history is framed around the rulers and politics of that particular time, but folklore offers another perspective. It gives us insight into the lives of the everyday people, people like us. As such, folklore contains the knowledge of those people, encoded in the form of myth and stories. In this way, it relates to our ancestors and is a means of spanning time and space to learn from them. Pure magic itself!

These stories are often wonderful and most definitely weird, which is no surprise and perhaps one reason why they are easily dismissed as tales told by worn-out mothers to scare unruly children into obedience. Yet, once you begin to scratch a little deeper than surface level, you begin to realise that they are not to be taken literally. Instead, their real messages and lessons are encoded in rich imagery and symbolism that speak to the human psyche. This allows us, the listener, to interact with the themes and contexts in a meaningful way that relates to our own lived experiences and ideas. Even today, such stories and themes play a massive part in our lives. It's what we do in our free time, our most precious time: we interact with stories that deal with themes as old as our very species. Just look how many TV shows, films, and novels impact our lives.

In looking a little deeper, in exploring the stories of our ancestors and the land, we can really begin to see just how much they not only inform our current understanding and knowledge of that land but enhance it. Such stories tell us so much, not only of the land itself and the changes that have occurred within those spaces over the many hundreds and thousands of years but also how our ancestors interacted with that land. In this way, you can begin to really see how much this informs your current understanding of place and space.

The UK's folklore around the elder tree is a good example of this. The elder was perhaps the first tree I began working with in a conscious way, other than using the berries and flowers in cooking. Maybe that's why I have a particular soft spot for this little tree.

The way my relationship with it began also significantly strengthened and deepened my attachment. My garden is beautiful, filled with mature trees, shrubs, and flowers. Among the massive linden and the beautiful cherry, hiding just behind the ivy, is a small elder tree.

I can't remember who made the comment now, but I was once told, "And that one, you want to cut that down, you know. It's not a real tree, more of a weed."

I remember thinking, What makes a proper tree? And who was to say this little tree wasn't one? And why? But then, it's what we have been conditioned to do, isn't it? How many useful plants are called weeds, a blight to be pulled up or doused in weed killer. If I'm honest, I felt bad for the tree, for nature as a whole for that matter. A throwaway comment by someone I can't even remember just seemed to sum up the general attitude towards and lack of care about the individual elements that make up nature as a whole.

Anyway, as I said, this marked the start of my relationship with the elder in a deeper way than just using it. I was already searching out recipes that featured the flowers and berries, and I also devoured any stories and lore I could find. Imagine how excited I was to discover its associations with witchcraft and magic! From the mundane act of cooking to the spiritual, the more I thought about it, the more I saw this process as a reciprocal one—a deepening of a spiritual, magical, and mundane symbiotic relationship. And this is what I absolutely love about folklore. It's as though the smallest and seemingly insignificant spark can set ablaze a passion you didn't know you had!

Let this feeling of excitement guide you!

Doing so will combine your learning with the practical doing that will, in turn, let you begin to really embed the learning from such lore and stories into your wider understanding of the land. This will ultimately add to and strengthen any relationships formed.

There are so many stories surrounding the elder, and the folklore is wonderfully varied. In some stories, the tree is benevolent and offers protection. In parts of the UK, people believed that planting a rowan (mountain ash) near the front of the property and an elder in the back would draw good fortune and ward off the bad. The elder does have fly-repelling properties, and bunches of it were hung up in cattle sheds and stables to protect against negativity and evil.

The elder is a tree of paradoxes. Believed to protect against witchcraft and magic, it was also believed that witches would and could turn into an elder tree as a disguise when needed. To prove it was a witch, all you had to do was cut any part of the tree and if it "bled" sap, then it was a witch.

In lore from Northampton, England, a story tells how a farmer who was out with his son one day, attempted to cut a branch from a tree to use as a walking stick. It wasn't any old tree, but an elder tree. So much sap bled from the cut, they couldn't continure cutting through the branch and so left it for a bad job. On the way home, the pair saw an old lady who just so happened to have a cut on her arm that wouldn't stop bleeding.

To add to the confusion, in some stories, witches weren't evil but were instead allies to those in power or the people in their communities. One such folk story explains how the Rollright Stones, a stone circle in Oxfordshire, England, came to be.

There was once a greedy and unjust king who wanted to become the ruler of the whole of England and so sought out the local witch for advice. She told the king all he desired would indeed come into being, but there was of course a catch:

> *Seven long strides shalt thou take,*
> *If Long Compton thou canst see,*
> *King of England thou shalt be.*[1]

In other words, all the king had to do was take seven long strides, and if he could see the village of Long Compton, then he would become king of all England. Thinking this an easy task, seeing as they were almost there anyway, the king took seven long strides. But the witch knew the land and knew that between them and the village was a mound that blocked the view. On the seventh step, she called out:

> *As Long Compton thou canst not see*
> *King of England thou shalt not be.*
> *Rise up, stick, and stand still, stone,*
> *For King of England thou shalt be none.*

---

1. Arthur J. Evans, "The Rollright Stones and Their Folk-Lore," *Folk-Lore* 6 (1895): 19.

Thou and thy men hoar stones shall be
And I myself an eldern-tree.[2]

And with that, the king and his soldiers were transformed into the standing stones. They are still there to this very day. And the witch? She, too, remains in the form of an elder tree, a protective guardian of that land and place.

And yet other lore deals with the spirit that resides within the tree, and these stories are some of my favourites. This spirit is often seen as an old woman called the Elder Mother in places such as Denmark and areas in Britain. In the next county over from mine, Lincolnshire, she is more often referred to as "the old girl" or "the old lady."

These stories, along with my own experiences with the tree, have helped me to develop an appreciation of it, one that extends much further than simply being grateful for the gifts of food and healing.

The acts can be small, such as simply spending time in the garden or nodding to the tree in recognition whenever you see it when you're out. You can even talk aloud to the tree. Combined with the collective knowledge of those who came before in the form of folklore, such simple acts can help to develop a meaningful practice that adds a rich depth to your witchcraft. I know they have done so for my own craft. More than that, though, it has made me see not only the tree but the indwelling spirit and has allowed me to build a relationship with it individually and in the wider aspect of the genius loci.

Types of Nature Spirits

The Elder Mother is a nature spirit, a nymph. The term *nymph* comes from the ancient Greeks, and we can find all manner of nymphs and stories concerning them woven into the rich tapestry

---

2. Evans, "The Rollright Stones and Their Folk-Lore," 19.

that is Greek mythology. Nymphs can be seen as the personification of natural forces, phenomena, beings, and objects. But this personification of such things and the stories that go with them can be seen not just in the history of the ancient Greeks, but of all peoples in all places. Cultures all over the world have their own rich history of stories and lore that seek to explain the connection with the natural world. Though the beings, terms, and names will undoubtedly be different—and rightly so too, after all, diversity is indeed the spice of life—humans across the globe have always been aware that the other beings we share the world with are alive with spirit. Though everything changes and is in constant flux, the spirits of the land remain.

If we wanted to be exact, the Elder Mother might best be described as a dryad, which is a tree nymph or spirit, and these were often depicted as beautiful women. While dryads were originally associated with the oak tree, the name evolved, becoming generalised across all tree species. Oak dryads are now known specifically as drys.

In counties of the UK such as Somerset that are renowned for their apple and pear orchards and cider production, it might come as no surprise that the spirit of the apple tree features in folklore from these regions. Aptly named, the Apple Tree Man is believed to be the indwelling spirit of the oldest apple tree in any given orchard. If honoured with a libation of cider poured at the roots, he will bring good fortune and prosperity in the form of an abundant harvest the following year.

In Haitian Vodou, Grand Bois is the Lwa associated with trees and plants. It's also interesting to note that a living tree can also be used as a *poto-mitan*, the central pillar or pole of the peristyle (temple), through which the Lwa traverses during ritual and worship. In Jamaica and other Caribbean islands where Obeah is practised, Sasabonsam is the lord of the forest, an ambivalent protector of the wild spaces. And in Celtic and Gaulish mythology, the goddess

Arduinna is heavily associated with the region known as Ardennes, which itself spans parts of Belgium, Luxembourg, France, and Germany. Perhaps a goddess of the hunt, she is also associated with the flora and fauna of the region.

While we can often get swept away with romantic and perhaps nostalgic ideas, all sepia toned and dripping honey, when it comes to nature spirits, it's important to remember that as with other types of spirit, nature spirits can be malevolent as well as benevolent, while some are just downright indifferent to us. In some northern and eastern parts of the UK, Jinny or Jenny Greenteeth is a water spirit particularly associated with deep, dank pools of water, like stagnant ponds. And she is the stereotypical hag too: all green skin and pointed teeth, a devourer of children. She drags them down to the bottom where, local variation depending, she locks them in her house or traps them in the long weeds. Either way, the outcome is the same: death by drowning followed by being eaten!

The folk stories associated with places like this, that involve monstrous beings, often act as warnings. Remember what I said about folk stories, myths, and lore being ways of encoding knowledge to pass on down to the next generation? Mothers would tell their babes these stories in the hopes of scaring them away from dangerous, deep water.

What is particularly interesting is that sometimes nature spirits, or spirits that we have come to think of as nature spirits, began as mere mortals. This is the case at Betws-y-Coed, Conway in Wales, where a particular waterfall is associated with a local lord, John Wynn. In one version, he got a little too amorous with a young serving girl. When the girl rejected his advances, the lord became enraged and killed her. In other stories, it was an affair of youth that got too complicated. Either way, the end result was the same, and he buried her in an alcove and bricked it up. However, whether tormented by his own conscience or the spectre of the young girl, he threw himself into Swallow Falls (perhaps a somewhat dramatised version of the story told to scare children away from the waters, as the truth is he gave a deathbed confession), where his spirit is said to remain, trapped.

There is a wealth of material surrounding nature spirits in folklore from all over the world; it is simply fascinating. Whether the lore of different cultures or your own, there is a beauty and intrigue in them all, and this demonstrates not only our shared history with the land but also reflects how we are still engaging with the land and the spirits that reside there. As important as all of this is, how can you relate it to and assimilate it into your own witchcraft practice?

Nature Spirits Today

The stories and lore about nature spirits arise through historical connections to the land but also our present-day connection to it. When we interact with the spirits of the land, when we honour them and respect them, we are also adding to the rich and varied tapestries woven and passed down from those who came before. We can gain a deeper understanding of the beings we share our space with, and in doing so, they get to know us too. A relationship is a two-way street, after all.

Don't get it wrong though; this doesn't mean that every time you see a tree, plant, or animal when you're out and about that you have to bring to mind everything you know about that particular being, or that you have to learn all of this by rote. What it does mean, though, is that when you do encounter them, you will know it more deeply. Think about it this way: When you see a good friend, do you instantly call to mind all the experiences you have had together, all the things you know about them? No, of course not! Instead, you know them so very well, understand them even. This familiarity is built on weeks, months, and years of getting to know them, of building that friendship, and it is this that informs your relationship with that person. It is the same with the land and with nature too.

It's natural that some plants, trees, and birds will hold special meaning for you, just like the elder, blackbird, and sparrow do for me. This is the real beauty of it all—this special connection that is meaningful in ways you might not even fully understand yourself; you just know it sings to your spirit.

Reintroducing Yourself

Going to those wild and idyllic spaces is fantastic. Who wouldn't want to visit them? They are beautiful. A large forest, ocean, or mountain are magically powerful places, but so too is the single tree that grows in a housing estate, hedgerow, or garden.

We often take the natural world for granted, particularly if we live in more urbanised areas. It can be difficult to see the nature that lives in those spaces alongside us. A large part of that is the romanticised idea of the wild woods and those other wild spaces, such as mountains and oceans. These have become the idealised aspects of nature, and anything else just won't cut it.

Exploration: The Land Around You

Go outside where you live and reconnect with nature and the land there. If you are able to visit different parts of your town or city, then great! If you can only manage to get out in your street or garden, then that, too, is good enough. If you absolutely cannot get outside for whatever reason, then sitting by an open window is perfectly fine. Witchcraft, as ever, is adaptable!

Make an effort to get out daily if you can. Try different times of the day and in all weathers too, no matter how uncomfortable. There is no such thing as unsuitable weather, only unsuitable clothing! Pay attention to what is growing where and when, the trees, the animals, how you feel and respond to the myriad stimuli our environments contain. Nothing exists in a vacuum.

Simply pay attention.

When you return, make notes in your journal. Take your time to explore your reactions to your experiences. It's okay if you don't fully understand your reactions and responses, but by making the time and space to explore them, you will gain insight and, over time, gain a deeper understanding of yourself and your connection to the land where you live.

Dedication and Intent

Now that you have already dipped your toe into the concept of rewilding and have started to explore your local landscape with new eyes, it's time to go a little deeper. You may have already begun to sense that feeling of connection between you, a space, and the other creatures and beings that share it with you. Just by making that effort to consciously spend time out in nature, you are already forging those connections with the land and the genius loci.

Now it is time to formally declare your intentions and purpose. The following ritual sets the energy for the work you are about to do and focuses your intent and will. It is a conscious commitment from you to the land.

Ritual: Dedication

If you feel comfortable enough to do this ritual outside, then go for it. A garden is perfect! However, if not, don't worry. You can go for a walk out in your local area beforehand or even just stand or sit on your doorstep. If you are doing this ritual inside, then have a window open to allow the fresh air in.

You can do this ritual whenever you want; the timing is not important other than making sure you have the time to do it. Bathe beforehand using products without heavy perfume or scent and wear comfortable clothes.

For this ritual, you will need:

- A white tealight candle
- A bowl of fresh water
- An offering of native wildflower seeds, birdseed, nuts, flower petals (any natural items that will benefit and not hinder wildlife)

There is no need to set sacred space. If you are outside, then this can be considered sacred already, and your home is your home. If you wish to tidy the area, then you can in your initial prep.

Set the items out on the ground with the candle in the centre, the water to one side, and the offering to the other.

When you are ready, light your candle. Sit in front of the items and allow yourself a few moments to acclimatise to your surroundings. Allow yourself to relax, and when you are ready, take a deep breath in and hold it for a count of four before exhaling completely. Repeat this twice more. Close your eyes and spend a moment or two becoming aware of any feelings and sensations around and within you.

Focus your attention on the journey ahead, your purpose of working with the land, and all you hope to achieve from building this relationship. You might see this as flashes of images; you may chant over and over your aims or whisper your intent.

When you are ready, take a moment to gather your thoughts in silence. Now speak aloud, whether a whisper or a cry. Call to the genii locorum, the nature spirits, and the spirits of place. State your intent to them, and ask for them to be present, to witness. Say whatever words are true and heartfelt; this is more important than poetic language and flowery imagery. When you have finished, spend a few moments in reflection and give your offerings, asking that the spirits of this place and land accept them. Pour the water as a libation. Tidy away all your belongings, blowing out the candle and allowing it to cool before disposing of it appropriately. Leave nothing but your offering.

Chapter 4
Songs of Day and Night

◆◆◆◆◆◆

Before we look at the songs of the seasons and the ways we can connect with the land and the genius loci throughout the turning of the wheel, it's a good idea to consider the smaller natural cycles.

Day and night, like the seasons, occur because of astronomical events. Day and night happen as the earth spins on its axis in its orbit around the sun. Where the earth is in its orbit will determine how many hours of light and dark we have.

Working with the cycles of day and night allows us as witches and occultists to have control of how and when we practise. Lots of spells and rituals often require you to work at a specific time or moon phase, and yet similar energies can be found at different times of the day. This allows us a greater deal of control over our workings and when we might perform them.

It is also another way you can begin to connect more with the natural world around you. Understanding these cycles and how they impact you, the world around you, and the other beings you share that space with is key in really developing a strong animistic practice. It's also important to remember connectivity and how everything is connected—as above, so below, as within so without. Think about it this way: if something has an effect on us as living beings with a soul, then surely those same occurrences are bound to affect other beings with a soul, other spirits. Of course, those effects will be different,

41

but it's important to consider them if we truly want to build a solid relationship.

Days of the Week

In classical astronomy, each day of the week is ruled by one of the seven classical planetary influences, these being Saturn, Jupiter, Mars, the Sun, the Moon, Venus, and Mercury:

- ◆ Monday: Moon
- ◆ Tuesday: Mars
- ◆ Wednesday: Mercury
- ◆ Thursday: Jupiter
- ◆ Friday: Venus
- ◆ Saturday: Saturn
- ◆ Sunday: Sun

While some of these associations may appear obvious, such as the Moon and Monday and Saturday and Saturn, others may seem a little more obscure. Again, this is one of those instances when having a deeper understanding of seemingly arbitrary and everyday occurrences can deepen and strengthen your connection to those times. Not only that, but names—including place names and more obviously the names given to each day of the week—tell us something of the history of the land and the peoples who may have called that place home once upon a time. Tuesday is named after the Norse god Tyr, Wednesday after the Roman god Mercury, but it also has links with the god Woden, a version of Odin. The Norse theme continues with Thursday being named after Thor (while also having links with the Roman god Jupiter), and Friday is named for Frigg (or the Roman goddess Venus).

By working with the days of the week and their planetary influences, we can utilise the energies and power associated with them, which can be found in the table below.

Planet	Associations and Correspondences
Moon	Magic, intuition, psychic abilities
Mars	Courage, boldness, directiveness, war, anger
Mercury	Abstract thinking, logic, communication, clarity, directiveness
Jupiter	Success, chance, work and careers, strength, concentration, focus
Venus	Love, romance, lust, beauty, good times, relationships
Saturn	Ambition, practicality, organisation, breaking habits, will
Sun	Career, success, clarity, authority, health

Planetary Hours

Not only are the days of the week governed by the seven planetary influences, but the hours of each day are too. This changes every day, as the hours are calculated using the sunrise and sunset times, but this needn't be overly difficult. Nowadays there are apps and websites available to us, so it needn't be any effort at all. Despite this ease though, I often think it's good form to have a basic understanding of how to calculate them yourself.

The first thing to remember is that the first hour of each day is ruled by the planet associated with that day, so for example, the first planetary hour of Monday is ruled by the Moon. The order of the planets is as follows: Saturn, Jupiter, Mars, Sun, Venus, Mercury, Moon. This cycle repeats throughout the day.

It's also important to understand that when we talk about the first hour, we do not mean the first hour of the new day, that time between midnight and one a.m. Instead, the sunrise is taken as the beginning of the day, and that first hour after sunrise is the first hour of the day. So for example, if the sunrise occurred at five a.m. on a Monday, then the hour between five and six is ruled by the Moon. The next hour would then be ruled by Saturn and so on through the cycle.

To complicate matters, planetary hours do not necessarily last an hour, owing to the fact they are dependent on the sunrise and sunset. Indeed, the only time when they would be sixty minutes in length would be at the equinoxes when day and night are equal in length.

To calculate the planetary hours for the daytime, all you need to do is add the hours between sunrise and sunset and divide by twelve. To calculate the planetary hours for the nighttime, you add the hours between sunset and sunrise and divide by twelve. As an example, let's say you want to calculate the planetary hours for a Monday when the sun rises at five a.m. and sets at seven p.m. This gives us fourteen hours of sunlight. We then convert this to minutes by multiplying by sixty. When we divide this by twelve, this gives us the length of each planetary hour: seventy minutes (14 hours of sunlight gives 840 minutes: $840 \div 12 = 70$ minutes). In this way, then, the first hour between five a.m. and sixteen minutes past six is governed by the Moon and lasts for seventy minutes. The next hour would then be Saturn, lasting for seventy minutes, followed by Jupiter, and so on through the cycle.

It might sound complicated, but when you break it down into these simple steps, calculating the planetary hours need not be a daunting task. And besides, there is no shame in using an app or the internet to find the information you need.

By using the planetary hours to plan your spells, rituals, and other workings, you can tap into a range of energies and associations without having to wait a week, month, or longer for a particular moment. The planetary hours also offer a lot of flexibility in that we can choose a time that not only fits in with the associations and correspondences we need, but also suits our own routines.

An often overlooked but yet important aspect of working with the planetary hours is that it directs our attention to the sunrise and sunsets. These are important times of the day and an obvious cycle that can help connect us to the land where we live. Even if you do not use that first or last planetary hour of the day, using the planetary hours at least gets us thinking about these times and how we can apply them to our own magical practices.

Sunrise, Sunset, Dusk, and Dawn

A simpler way of working with the daily cycles of the sun is to observe and utilise the significant parts of the day, such as sunrise and sunset as well as dawn and dusk.

These times are special and significant because they are liminal and transitory, and as such they are potent and can enhance spellwork and ritual.

Oftentimes, the terms *sunrise* and *dawn* are used interchangeably, as are *dusk* and *sunset*, however there is a difference between these terms, though it is correct they are associated with one another and are often worked with simultaneously.

Dawn is the morning twilight period, that transition between dark and light before the sunrise. The *sunrise* occurs the exact moment the sun starts to rise in the sky, breaking the horizon. On the other end, then, *dusk* is the evening twilight, while *sunset* is the moment the sun slips below the horizon.

At these times of being in between day and night, light and dark, there is a special power that can be tapped into and utilised. It is worth spending some time observing the sunrise and sunsets, the dawn and the dusk to get a feel for these times and the energies that arise at each. It might require a little extra effort depending on the time of year and how early the sunrise is, but it will be well worth the effort, as you will feel firsthand just how different these times are.

Because these are transitional times, they are potent for magic that is geared towards some kind of change or shift. Dawn is good to get a feel for the energies just as the day is beginning to unfurl. This is potent energy for workings that require growth. The sunrise is a good time for workings with a specific aim that harnesses the power of that instant, the crowning of a new day, filled with the promise of possibility. At dusk, the day is winding down. This is a good time for working on the self, restorative work, and healing work. Sunset is a good time for transformational work within the self, what might be termed *shadow work*.

If you can get outside at these times, even better; however, do not despair if you don't have a safe outdoor space. You can stand or sit by your open front door for a few minutes or open a window and just sit with the lights off and the window open so that you can see how the light changes as dawn ascends and the sun rises.

There is indeed a special magic to these moments of the day, and being aware of them, experiencing them firsthand, is a great way of beginning to incorporate them into your witchcraft practice.

Noon

Like midnight, noon is also easy to overlook and miss because of the lack of visual reminders, but also because most of us are busy in the middle of the day. However, with noon, you at least get two chances to observe it. If we go by the clock, then noon is midday, twelve o'clock in the afternoon on the dot. But there is also high noon, and for this we do not need a clock. *High noon* simply refers to the time at which the sun is at its highest point in the sky, and this changes throughout the year depending on the season and where you are in the world.

Noon always feels less dramatic than midnight, or at least that's how it seems to me. I suppose this is in part because I'm often asleep at midnight unless I make an effort to stay up for it. Another reason is because noon always seems so matter of fact. It reminds me of the Sun (XIX) in the tarot. At noon, the sun is directly overhead, so there are no shadows or they are very short. Nothing can hide, and you can see everything clearly, the good and the bad. This is the energy that abounds at noon. Think of the sun at noon on a summer's day, bright and strong, with the promise of growing stronger still. There is an air of possibility, but this is tempered by the clarity and logic that comes with being aware, of seeing things clearly.

By bringing this understanding and clarity into our witchcraft in an animistic way, we come to respect and worship nature as it is, not romanticised nor misunderstood or made to feel small and less important.

Visualisation

Visualisations are a great way of tapping into the power and energy of the sunrise and sunset. Similar to a guided meditation in that they ask you to imagine, to visualise a specific scenario, visualisations are much shorter and so offer versatility when it comes to time constraints.

I like to use visualisations in several ways. Whenever I am doing a working or ritual for a specific outcome, visualisation is a great tool for directing the will towards the desired outcome. It's also a good way to evoke a particular feeling, which is useful in spell work for stimulating power through emotions and feelings.

These sunrise, noon, and sunset visualisations will allow you to draw on your experiences of these sun cycles, which in turn allows you the time and space to process them more deeply.

Visualization: Sun Cycles

When getting started, don't get too hung up on exact timings; it's more important you do the visualisation. Of course, that doesn't mean the effort shouldn't be made to do the visualisations as close to the times they represent as possible, but if you're an hour after sunrise or you don't get a lunch break until after noon, then it's no big deal. The important thing is that you do them. And as these visualisations will take as little as three minutes, it should be easy to fit them into even the busiest of schedules. It will be worth the effort; you'll see! If you wish to record the visualisations to play back during the actual exercise, then you can. This is particularly good if you have constraints on your time that limit how long you can engage in the activity for; however, they can be done as needed so as long as you have an idea of what the aim is and are familiar with the feelings and energies you are trying to evoke. In this case, reading through the visualisations until you are familiar with them will help keep them in mind.

For each visualisation, get into a comfortable position and minimise any distractions and disruptions. After each, have a drink of water, and then normal service can resume. Alternatively, if you have the time and wish to do a working, spell, or ritual to coincide with any of the times, you can use the required visualisation to invoke the power and energy to imbue your work.

Sunrise:

Close your eyes.

In your mind's eye, see yourself outside in a place of meaning to you. It might be a beach or a forest. You might see yourself on a mountain or even just in your own garden.

Dawn has broken and the sun is moments from creeping above the horizon. Already the sky is a bright splash in the east against an ever-brightening backdrop.

As the sun rises, feel the energies of the land, of the sun. Feel the awakening and restorative power of the sunrise.

Concentrate on the feelings it inspires within you and the land.

Feel the power of the sunrise fill you. It feels like pale gold.

Feel it within you.

See it reflected in the land.

Noon:

Close your eyes.

Visualise the sun, high in the sky. Bright and hot.

Feel the sunlight on your skin and feel your skin react to this hot energy.

Feel the energy of the noon sun, strong and hot. It flows into you, filling you until you are totally full with the power and energy of the bright noon sun.

It feels as though there is nothing you cannot achieve. Everything is visible; you can see everything in high definition.

Feel the energy of the midday sun as it flows inside of you. See it reflected in the land around you.

Sunset:

Close your eyes.

Visualise yourself standing outside in a place that is special to you. It could be a forest, a beach, your own garden.

The day is drawing to a close, the sun already low in the sky. See the sky aflame with colour: reds, pinks, oranges deepening to purple.

Watch as the sun sinks lower and lower still until it is a splash of colour on the horizon, glowing like the embers of a dying fire.

Notice how the shadows stretch as nightfall descends.
Feel the energy of the sunset. Calming.
The sunset gives permission.
It is okay to relax, to take time for yourself, to turn your gaze inwards.
Feel the energy of the sunset inside of you.
See it in the land around you.

◆ ◆ ◆

Try and do these visualisations at least once a week, though effort should be made to do them daily. Once you get used to including them in your daily routine, it is easy to maintain the practice. These visualisations, because they are so quick and easy to do, are a great way to begin developing a daily practice if you do not already have one.

Midnight

Midnight is also a powerful time of day just as noon is, and it is essential we spend as much time exploring these as we do the others in order to get a fuller understanding of the cycles and rhythms of the day.

Midnight is steeped in folklore and myth. It is the witching hour, the time when devils and demons roam the earth and witches fly to sabbat upon the backs of goats. It is the time to go to the crossroads with a handful of pennies and a cigarette if you want your deepest desires to come true.

Midnight spent with friends at a party or a nightclub can often pass unnoticed. It's not like dawn or dusk, when the growing or fading light is visibly noticeable. However, when you make the effort to stay up, alone or with a small, quiet group all intent on the same purpose, then you will notice the quiet but heavy power of this liminal time.

Midnight is extremely powerful and can be used in workings for a variety of purposes, but especially those involving major transformation. Midnight is literally 00:00 (or 12:00 using a traditional clock), the moment when one day ends and the next begins. If you can, it's worth trying to experience this outside; however, if this cannot be done safely then it is enough to stand or sit by an open window with the lights off. As an alternative, try sitting with a lit candle at midnight.

While midnight might be considered a man-made invention in that it relies on the concept of time, it is still important in relation to animism and connection to the land. It's important to recognise how humans interact with one another and, more than that, to recognise that the cycles of those interactions do in fact impact the land and the other beings that reside there. At midnight, especially if you are at home or in a quiet street or rural area, chances are that at this time of night, there will be far fewer people around. There will also be less noise and light pollution. Because it is so quiet, in terms of human activity at least, you can often interact with the land and the spirits that reside there in a way that is unaffected by the energies and actions of other people. It feels more intimate, more meaningful.

Midnight workings, whether spell, ritual, or meditation, will need some prior planning, especially if you are usually tucked up in bed at this time of night. Unlike dusk and dawn, when time is less of an issue, for midnight workings, you really want to capture the energy that abounds. However, much like dusk and dawn, this energy doesn't just come and go within that very minute when the clock strikes twelve, but rather there is a building and receding of energies.

The energy of midnight can be quite frightening at first, especially if you do venture outdoors. Like most things, the unfamiliar can feel scary until it becomes more known, and acknowledging this is an important part of the journey, this recognition of our own feelings in relation to the land, particularly when those feelings are not expected or might be seen as "negative." This work of overcoming our own biases, fears, and all those other internal issues that hold us back from fulfilling our potential is extremely important and is what is meant, at least in part, by the term *shadow work*. Midnight is the perfect time for this work.

But fear is only one aspect of midnight, one that comes from the self rather than from the land. We often think of midnight, or indeed that space of hours commonly termed "the middle of the night," as being a time of quiet solitude and rest, and indeed it is … for us as humans. But what about the land itself? At midnight, the dark is like a cloak. At first glance, all is hidden beneath the dark ruffles and layers, but it's not only our eyes that need to get used to the dark of midnight. Before long, your other senses, including those that fall outside of the common five, will tune in to the night, and it is as though that dark cloak slips away, revealing a nighttime alive and potent.

Midnight is the time of secretiveness, when we slip into the world unpopulated by humans, unseen. It is the traditional time associated with witches and witchcraft purely because of that secretive air. But it is also a time of deep and poignant energy: think of the dance between hunter and prey and how that feeds into the cycles of life and death. The call of the owl or the screech of the fox. These sounds bring to mind the essence of this time—the fear, the act of moving consciously through the dark, of magic itself.

Exercise: Sensory Midnight

Unless you're something of a night owl, by the time midnight rolls around, chances are you will be in bed, either asleep or about to be. Either way, most of us don't make a special effort to sit up and wait for midnight to just experience it.

As we have already touched upon, at this time of night, when there is less human activity and the outside world can seem strange, even familiar places can feel so totally different. This aims to allow us to use our senses to explore this time. In doing so, we will be able to form a connection with the land in a more intimate way, which is indeed apt for the time.

With that said, you will need to do this at midnight, and so you may require some time to plan how you will achieve this if you are normally fast asleep at this time. Will it be better to stay up, maybe having a nap earlier on in the day? Or maybe it's better to set your alarm a little before the time? These are questions you will need to figure out, and it is worth trying a couple of ways and seeing which works best for you. Which makes you feel more comfortable and alert?

For this, if you have a garden or a space outside somewhere that you will feel safe, then I encourage you to do this there. However, having such a space and being able to access it may not be appropriate for everyone, and if this is the case, then an alternative is to do it inside in a room with the lights off and the windows open.

To begin, sit or stand comfortably with your eyes closed and just breathe normally. Allow yourself a couple of moments to just let your body settle and attune to your surroundings.

Be aware of your body and slowly allow your consciousness to move gently past your body. You might concentrate on the ground beneath you or the cool night air on any exposed skin. Perhaps a breeze ruffles your hair and raises goosebumps.

Take a deep breath and then another. Notice how the night air tastes different from the air in the day. What else do you notice? How does it differ?

Now listen. Try not to think about or analyse the sounds you hear, instead simply acknowledge them. Perhaps it's the wind through the tree-tops or the crackle of twigs and leaves as any small night creatures go about their business. Perhaps, if it is the right season or time of year, you can hear the flutter of wings as moths and other insects pass close by.

As you are listening and allowing yourself to feel the sensations of being outside, or even just aware of your midnight surroundings, allow yourself to build a mental picture of them. Try to hold this picture in your mind's eye. (If you are artistically minded, you may wish to produce a sketch of what your mind's eye sees.)

When you are ready, open your eyes and go through the same process of sending forth your consciousness further outside of your body and into your surroundings. Notice as your eyes get used to the darkness. What can you see and hear? How does this feel different to the daytime? When you have finished, spend some time making notes in your journal. I find it helpful to do this, as it gives me the time and space to really explore my experiences, and it is a great way to draw a deeper understanding of them.

Chapter 5
Songs of the Moon

◆◆◆◆◆◆

The moon and witchcraft go together like, well, the moon and witchcraft! There is no escaping the fact that the moon plays a pretty big part in many magical traditions and paths. And it's not surprising that we should consider the moon and the lunar cycles in relation to animism and living in a way that is more in tune with nature and the spirits that reside there.

We already know that the moon affects the natural world here on earth. We know that the moon affects water and the tides. Although there are no clear scientific links that prove the moon's effect on our moods and behaviour, many people claim to feel different around the time of the full moon. And as someone who works with children in an educational setting, many of my colleagues and I swear blind that the full moon does indeed affect the children's behaviour.

Whether you're a lunar sceptic, seeing the moon as a pretty rock that just so happens to orbit our planet, or you truly believe the moon has the power to affect us, the fact is that the moon is as much a part of nature as anything else we shall consider throughout the course of this book. Understanding the lunar energies throughout the different parts of its cycle and how they affect us both physically and magically can have an impact on our witchcraft practices.

Moon Folklore

All cultures, it would seem, have stories, myths, and legends relating to the moon. Sometimes these stories are fun, such as the classic tale that it's made from cheese, others are more poignant like the story of the man in the moon, and then there's everything in between!

Representing Knowledge and Understanding

In many ways we can see the moon as representing knowledge. Let's take the tarot for instance. The Moon in the tarot speaks of a different type of knowledge to that presented in the Sun card. Whereas the harsh noon sun allows us to see everything clearly, warts and all, the light of the moon is more mystical and intuitive. I believe this is embodied in the familiar imagery of the moon-gazing hare, which itself is associated with possibility, fortune, growth, and rebirth. None of these things come about without knowledge. But it is more than simply acquiring that knowledge. It's how you use that knowledge, how you apply it, that makes the real difference, and the moon allows us to view things in a different way from the harsh, no-nonsense manner of the sun.

The Moon as Protector

When we consider the moon in relation to many of the deities associated with it, quite often the theme of protection comes up. From Ishtar to Artemis, many of the deities offer protection to their worshippers while also offering some protection or service to the moon.

While researching local folklore, I stumbled on a local story found in a larger collection of stories: "Legends of the Cars" by M. C. Balfour. This story, too, sees the moon as protector of the land but also shows the reciprocal nature of the relationship between ourselves and the land.

"The Dead Moon" (also called "The Buried Moon" in other versions and collections) tells of the moon as protector of the land, particularly of the carrs. A carr is a type of boggy wood, and this particular one was safe to travel in those nights when the moon's silver glow bathed the land. But on dark nights, all manner of evil and mischievous creatures stalked the carr.

Hearing stories about the creatures that roamed the dark woods, the moon donned a cloak of darkest night and slid beneath the boughs to catch a glimpse. But the moon became tangled in its robes and slipped into the carr, becoming stuck beneath the murky waters. Struggle as it might, it was stuck steadfast.

All the while, a traveller, thinking the moon would be high in the sky, entered the carr and soon became lost. He could hear the creatures, bogles and worse, stalking him in the undergrowth, and his unease soon turned to fear.

Hearing him pass close by, the moon renewed its struggles and for an instant, the cloak slipped away, revealing the moon's bright light. Although it only lasted a brief moment, it was enough to frighten away the creatures, allowing the man to make it to the village safely. There he told the villagers all that had befallen him on his journey, and they set off into the carr to search for the moon. Of course, they found and helped the moon, and it returned to its rightful place, serving as protector of the land once more, but this time also as the protected—or, rather, saved.[3]

This story hints at the reciprocal relationship between humans and nature, this time nature being represented by the moon. Though folk stories are often simple and fantastical at the same time, they allow us to explore the seemingly separate parts of the world and see that we are not separate at all.

---

3. M. C. Balfour, "Legends of the Cars." *Folk-Lore* 2, no. 2 (June 1891): 157–164.

The Importance of the Lunar Cycle

We often think of numbers, patterns, and that sort of thing as human inventions, don't we? Mathematical occurrences are named after the men who discovered them—think Pythagoras's theorem $(a^2+b^2=c^2)$. No wonder we don't really come to think of such things as belonging to and in nature.

Nature is full of patterns and cycles, from the formation of rocks and minerals to the seasons, from the phases of the moon to menstruation. While one could indeed consider all of these things through the lens of animism, for now we will concentrate on the moon because of its obvious links to magic and witchcraft. The moon is also accessible to everyone. You don't need to be initiated into any tradition or practice; you need no tools. All that is needed to make a rudimentary study of the moon and its cycles is yourself and the time to simply watch and observe.

The moon's cycle can be broken down into many parts, but for our purposes, all we really need to be able to do is identify the dark moon, the new moon, the full moon, the waning moon, and the waxing moon.

The moon orbits the earth and takes roughly 28 days, while its phases take a little over 29 days to complete. It is the sun's reflection falling on the moon that gives us the different phases in this approximately 29-day cycle

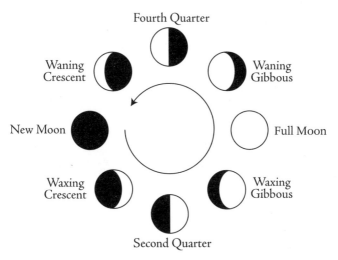

Fourth Quarter

Waning Crescent

Waning Gibbous

New Moon

Full Moon

Waxing Crescent

Waxing Gibbous

Second Quarter

Figure 2: Moon Phases Graphic

The Dark Moon

I might be splitting hairs here; for indeed, some do regard this as part of the new moon. However, I consider the time when no part of the moon is visible in the sky an important time with its own energy and power. Not only does it mark the end of the cycle and the beginning of the next, making it a liminal time, it is also significant magically and spiritually.

The dark moon is a time of honesty; it is the darkness of the confession booth, though there is no sin here. The dark can be a comfort, especially in difficult times, and there is nothing more difficult than honesty, even when we are alone. The dark moon is the time to speak out to the genii locorum, the local nature spirits. You might feel self-conscious doing this, but you'll soon get over that feeling. Introduce yourself. Believe it or not, you have already made the connections if you have worked through the previous sections of this book. Spirit recognises spirit, after all. The point here, though, is to continue forging that connection by stating aloud your intentions, of speaking to the spirits directly, whether you feel them there or not. Chances are, you will need to do this a few times until you start feeling comfortable, so don't worry if on your first attempt you don't feel any connection to the spirits or you feel a little bit daft and self-conscious. We have to work through our own blockages and issues, one of which can be speaking aloud to spirits without feeling a little silly. Do not underestimate the conditioning we all have; it can take a while to push these things to the side.

Visualisation: Dark Moon

This is where your experiences will be important. If you haven't consciously worked with the dark moon as a distinct part of the cycle, then it is well worth spending a little time and effort to go outside or by an open window during this phase. Simply begin by observing the night sky with no moon. Perhaps the stars seem brighter. And what about the feelings stirred within you during this time? Do you feel it's time to work on yourself, to turn that dark gaze inwards and scry your own soul? Maybe you feel all of these things and more, or maybe you feel none of them. This is precisely why it is important to work with your own associations, to draw on your own experiences.

So now that you have at least a little experience of what the night feels like when the moon is dark, it's time to consider how these experiences can form a part of your visualisation.

In a visualisation, you are bringing to the very forefront of your consciousness the feelings and atmosphere of whatever it is you hope to emulate or recreate. You might do this in a variety of ways, relying on images and sounds and not just a spoken narrative.

To begin, close your eyes and see yourself immersed in the land, somewhere meaningful to you, such as a garden, by a tree, or even somewhere more urban. Bring to mind all of those thoughts, feelings, and happenings that you have felt or witnessed there. Maybe there is a deep peacefulness or the scurrying of night critters. At first, it is worth just being in this space. When you feel comfortable with this, consider and bring forth all those aspects the dark moon brings, such as the inner reflection, quietness, and darkness. What does it add to this space? How does it change you, which in turn may change how you interact with this space? Whenever I do this visualisation, it's almost as if I can see elements of myself reflected in the land, as though the dark moon gives me the space and safety to really explore the shadows of self through my connection to the land. In this way, the genii locorum can become those archetypal figures that help us to understand the world around us and our place within it.

The beauty of this particular visualisation is that it is constantly changing and shifting because it is firmly rooted in your own experiences.

The New and Waxing Moon

Some people do include the dark moon in this phase; however, I see the new moon as starting as soon as the moon begins to show, about a day after the dark moon. There is something exciting about the appearance of that first bright sliver, and it is a potent time in terms of performing magic and ritual associated with new beginnings and for adding driving force to any working.

As the moon continues through its cycle, that first thin sliver gradually gets bigger, growing larger in the night sky. As the moon grows in stature, so too does it grow in power, and so the waxing moon is great for spells and rituals associated with growth, fortune, and generally attracting or growing.

At the dark moon, you were encouraged to speak aloud to the genii locorum. Now as the new moon appears in the sky and continues to grow, it's about building on those foundations. You've done the hard part, made easier by the cloak of darkness, and so now it's about growing those relationships and accepting the personal growth that comes with them.

Exploration: The Night

The new moon leading into the waxing moon is also an auspicious time for starting something new. This makes it the perfect time to begin a real study of the land and the spirits. Spending time outside in those spaces that are familiar in the daytime is a good way to gain a dual understanding of those places. It gives you a clearer, fuller experience of the whole.

It's a good idea to try and get out at the same time each evening or night if possible. This will allow you to get used to that area and so allow for a greater awareness of any changes that occur through the growing of the moon as it passes through its cycle.

Notice where the moon is at this time and how it moves through the sky each night. What about the stars? Can you see Jupiter rising? Pay attention to the land as well. Do some nights feel different to others? How so? Can you see any differences in the activities of animals, or does the night take on a different feel or energy?

All of these observations will give you the time and space to explore the land through this phase of the moon. While observing might seem something of a passive activity, it shouldn't be. To truly observe means to be present in the moment in a variety of ways. It's about being conscious of the goings on around you without interfering or centring the self while also being an active part of that landscape. It's about allowing yourself to be moved by the same energies that stir in the land and the beings around you and to which you are connected. It is about being honest and putting aside logic and reason, about experiencing without questioning your feelings or reactions while also being aware of them.

The Full Moon

It takes about two weeks from the dark moon for the moon to reach the peak of its orbit, when it appears full and round in the night sky. The full moon is steeped in myth, magic, and folklore and has a long history of being associated with witches as they danced with the devil at sabbat. Any kind of magic can be performed at the full moon, as it amplifies all energies.

Visualisation: Full Moon

This visualisation allows you to absorb the energies of the full moon whenever you need them. As with the previous dark moon visualisation, this should be governed by your own experiences. It's a good idea to begin to adapt the workings in this book to suit your own circumstances and experiences, as they will differ from my own. If you are new to witchcraft and magic, I suggest trying things as they are suggested first, as this allows you to get familiar with the routine of it and will highlight any areas you need to adapt.

When you are ready, sit in a comfortable position and close your eyes. Breathe naturally and just allow a couple of moments for your body to relax. When you are ready, take a deep breath and imagine you are outside at nighttime beneath the full moon. You can feel the energy of the moon. It's soft and gentle but thrums with power. It is potent but not overpowering. Visualise this energy as a soft, silvery light, cool and refreshing, like having a cold drink on a hot day. Feel this power, this energy, flow into you. It enters through the head, through the third eye. Feel it as it flows into you, filling you entirely. Feel the energy within you. You are strong and powerful, filled with the energy of the full moon. When you feel ready, open your eyes. You can do this short visualisation anytime you wish to harness the power of the full moon.

Exercise: Full Moon Spirit Work

At the dark moon you began speaking aloud to the genii locorum, the nature spirits that reside where you do. Now is the time to not only continue with that but to add to the practice. It's worth taking time to look back through your journal to refresh your memory about your experiences. The light glow of the moon is a different energy from the bold gaze of the noon sun, and so the full moon is a good time for reflection and also communication.

For this exercise, you will need:

- A white candle, any type you have on hand
- A bowl of water to offer to the land at the end of the exercise
- Your journal

First, spend some time outside, preferably at night, in quiet contemplation. Then return inside, if necessary, or stay outside for the remainder of the exercise. Next, take your bowl of fresh water and candle. Speak out to the genii locorum as you have been doing. Speak earnestly and from the heart. When you have finished, light the candle and sit before the bowl of water. Lose yourself in its reflection. By focusing on the surface of the water, not only is it a way of divining meaning or communication from any spirit, but it is also a way of quieting the mind, or at least that part of it that is always chattering, always looking for something to focus on and explore.

Oftentimes in any kind of occult or magical work, this part of the mind can be the biggest barrier. There will be times when you might start to doubt yourself, will perhaps tell yourself you are imagining any kind of responses, but again, this is something that you will have to work at to overcome, and this can be done simply by persevering with this exercise every full moon.

The Waning Moon

During this phase, the moon begins to diminish until it ends the cycle. The waning moon is a time associated with more malevolent works of magic but is also a time of rest, recuperation, and self-care. This energy is echoed in the land, and during the time of the waning moon, you can work with the genii locorum to bring those same energies into the self.

It's a good idea to continue with the work started at the new and waxing moons in order to give a good contrast of experience. This will allow you to compare the energies of these different moon phases, which are often seen as being the opposite of one another. It might be an idea to keep a journal or make a dream or vision board during these times to highlight your experiences of each. This way you will have a physical record that you will be able to study and look back on.

While the accepted associations may well suit the majority, you may find there are some discrepancies with how you feel or how the land responds to the moon phases.

Because this moon phase is generally one associated with self-care, it's a potent time to begin to think about your experiences with the land so far, to use the soft and slow energies of the waning moon to assimilate and consolidate your experiences into your practice. For some aspects, this might lead to new areas of discovery or highlight further areas of exploration. For others, this assimilation might be more practical, such as finding ways to make working with the moon more accessible to you. Keeping in mind the ultimate aim of deepening your relationship with the land, and the spirits of that land will allow you to come at the issue of moon worship from a different perspective, one that unifies all of those different and seemingly separate areas of magic.

Exercise: Observing the Lunar Cycle

Today, astrology is a big part of witchcraft for many people. Indeed, a search of hashtags on social media sites such as Instagram and Pinterest will throw up hundreds of hits showing all things astrology. While this can be a very useful thing, do not let what can be extremely complicated put you off working with the moon. One of the most powerful things you can do to become more familiar with the cycle and phases of the moon is to simply make an observation of them.

Most calendars and diaries include the moon phases, and if not, there are loads of really useful apps and websites that will give you the exact phase. The key is to remember to use them. (This might sound silly, but trust me, I've lost count of how many times I've missed a moon phase by a day or two because I've been too busy to notice.) Write them on a calendar or somewhere you are likely to see them. Adding reminders to your email and your phone will ensure you have a loud and persistent reminder!

Start at the beginning of the cycle. You can decide whether this means the dark moon or the new moon for you. For each phase, spend some time outside if you can. If this just isn't possible, then sit in front of an open window where you can see the moon.

Watch the moon. Lose yourself in it. Notice the landscape and how the moon affects it. Does it make the night brighter or more shadowy? Do you feel different with the different phases? If so, how? Does the land feel different and in what way? Does this affect you and how? Take note of how you feel not only while taking part in this exercise, but also at different times. Does the phase of the moon affect your sleep? Do you feel more energetic at certain phases and tired at others?

Make notes of all these things in your journal. By reflecting on your experiences, you will deepen your understanding of how the moon affects the land as well as yourself and how in turn your actions affect the different parts of your life, including your witchcraft practice and your spirituality. This is a reciprocal process, one that vibrates through the different realms and spaces, including the spiritual. Indeed, the moon is a great symbol of how the mundane, magical, and spiritual are all interlinked in many and varied ways. All of this feeds into developing an embodied and active relationship with nature and the genii locorum. It's also a great way of developing your skills around relaxing into the environment, of coming to accept that you are a part of it and not separate from it, as well as coming to understand yourself and the different ways you draw information from your surroundings and assimilate it into your lived experiences.

Chapter 6
Songs of Spring

◆◆◆◆◆◆

Spring is the traditional season of hope. Creatures stir and begin to wake from their winter's slumber; the days grow longer and warmer, though imperceptibly at first, mirrored in the bright yellow of early daffodils and the heady perfume of hyacinths carried on the wind.

In my small slice of the world, spring starts cold and frosty but by the end is almost summerlike. It is a season of drastic change and transformation, particularly as the energies warm and quicken.

Spring brings with it the sabbats Ostara and Beltane, both very much associated with emerging as though from a deep slumber and the natural urges that bring forth new life.

When I was a child, spring always meant blossom. When spring rolled around and everything began to grow back all green shoots and blossoms, the trees and gardens were like little oases of life brimming with nature among the concrete—in spite of it, perhaps. It was like drinking the coolest, cleanest water on a hot day. It's refreshing and energising.

One of my favourite trees on the estate had pink blossoms, and I think it stood out to me because most of the trees had white flowers. The pink blossoms grew so thick that the boughs looked as though they were covered in candyfloss.

The emergence of the blossoms always filled me with a sense of magic and joy, and indeed still does. I have a cherry tree in my garden at the front of my house, and every year it flowers, thick clusters of the softest, creamy-white cherry blossoms. It is so beautiful you could lose yourself simply by looking at the perfectly delicate blooms. It's hard to imagine that anything could be so beautiful, and it genuinely leaves you with a sense of wonder and awe at the magnificence of nature. I challenge anyone to sit beneath a tree in blossom and not become entranced, their woes forgotten if only for a moment.

It is the blossoms and the feelings they evoke that are the essence of spring. There's an air of hope and possibility. There's an energy in the air as everything begins to stir and grow, all green shoots and new leaves. Daffodils and snowdrops, and later on wild violets and tulips, bloom. Bright frosty mornings when winter's breath still lingers in the air but there's no bite to its bark, all against the musical backdrop that is the dawn chorus.

Awakenings

In response to these seasonal changes, many people find they, too, feel more optimistic, hopeful, and energetic. Perhaps it's just the lengthening daylight hours or the milder weather, who knows. But it seems to me that what is happening in nature happens inside of us too. An awakening, if you will.

As above, so below. As without, so within.

You know, that tree with the pink blossoms still grows on the estate. I walked past it not too long ago and paused for a moment, letting my hand trail across the rough bark. It's a small, stunted tree standing alone, definitely not what might be considered a fine specimen, nor beautiful in any way save for the way all trees are. And yet those things don't matter. When I recall that tree from my childhood, I only see its beauty in the thousands of pink blossoms and can only remember the happiness that beauty inspired within me. Now looking back, I think I also recognised the strength of spirit within that tree and within nature itself, the strength of spirit to survive in imperfect conditions and still be strong, to still be beautiful.

For the animist witch, working with the potent energies and the genius loci at this time of the year can help boost workings that involve growth, activity, and progression.

Exploration: Just Being

If you haven't already started making more of an effort to spend time outside, then spring is a good time to start as the weather begins to improve. It is a real eye-opener when you begin to take active notice of the changes that occur throughout the season, and it really does highlight the transformative power of spring.

To begin, choose one spot. It might be a tree, a garden, or even a local park. Next, sit there. That's it! By sitting and observing the same area over a period of time, you begin to develop familiarity. You might start out watching what happens over the course of a week, then building it up. If you are particularly drawn to art, you might wish to make several sketches of that area to show the changes. If not, writing them down in your journal along with any observations you've noticed about yourself and how you feel is also a good way of documenting said changes.

Of course, what you are really doing by sketching or writing is noticing those small details. You are making a direct effort to seek them out: the subtle way the light changes as the days lengthen, the different shades of verdant greens against the now-passed winter's backdrop of browns and greys, the signs of increased bird activity. In noticing these details along with the more obvious signs of spring, you are becoming more intimately involved in the landscape. You no longer feel like a guest but instead begin to feel a familiarity or a closeness. That some door has opened to you, through which you have stepped and now stand just inside the threshold, no longer an outsider but a welcome guest.

As you spend time outside, allow yourself to relax, to feel your own spirit rise and mingle with that of the land around you. Allow yourself to feel connected, to feel the energies you see around you and feel those same energies within you. This can often sound like poetic nonsense, but I have seen all too often how many times people talk themselves out of their feelings and experiences. Signs of this might include feelings of guilt for taking the time for yourself, feeling silly, as though you are making it up, or simply just doubting your experiences. This is something many people go through, often in bursts. It takes a lot of energy and patience to work through our own mental blocks and defence mechanisms, and spending time in nature can be a great way of doing this in a healing and transformative way.

Learn to recognise these feelings that being connected to the land inspires within you, both in body and mind. Practice trying to embody or evoke these feelings when you are at home or away from your outside space. Being able to bring up this energy as and when you need it will add great potency to your spellwork and rituals.

Ostara (21st–22nd March) ~ The Spring Equinox

Ostara occurs in March, but even before we get to the actual date of the spring equinox, we can feel these energies beginning to stir. Equinoxes occur twice a year: now in the spring, and again in autumn. At both times the sun is directly over the equator. As such, there is a balance of light and dark, night and day. In spring, this occurs when the sun is directly above the equator as the earth makes its way towards the most northern part of its orbit.

There are many theories about the origins of Ostara and who or what is worshipped. *Ostara* sounds so much like *Easter* that it is an obvious link to make between the two celebrations, especially when you consider the imagery associated with both, such as eggs, fertility, and so on. One theory is that as Christianity spread to new lands, it often swallowed up local practices and shrouded them in the Christian mythos, and Ostara is one such celebration. Other theories hint the name Ostara is linked to the Anglo-Saxon goddess Eostre. This goddess represented new beginnings and the spring, and her name is also similar to the Christian celebration of Easter.

What is obvious, what all of these theories and origin stories show us, is that the energies that abound at this time are felt by many peoples in many places. If these feelings, this recognition of the awakening earth, are not important, why are there so many stories, myths, legends and lore that seek to explain them?

To me, this again highlights the connection between us and the land and our place within nature. And besides, regardless of the beliefs surrounding this particular sabbat, one thing about which there can be no debate is the astronomical event that is the spring equinox.

All of this means Ostara is a good time to pause for a moment in this season that seems to be moving at lightning speed and really take the time to dive into building that connection to the land. It's about pausing for just a moment to actually enjoy the season. And there is lots to enjoy too. The more time you spend outside at this time, the more you will come to recognise what Ostara looks like in the land where you live. There might be common elements, events that are similar to my own, but there will also be so much more that is unique to your small slice of the world.

The Dawn Chorus

At Ostara, the dawn chorus is at its peak as the bird mating season kicks off in full swing. If you can get up at sunrise, even if it's just once a week, it is more than worth doing, and you will be glad you took the time to make the effort. It's easy to get into a routine, and it's a great start to the day. I take my morning coffee outside every day as soon as I wake up. I like to simply sit and enjoy the early morning before the rest of the world awakens. There is so much magic to be found in the birdsong and the simple, quiet beauty of a day beginning to unfold. It's this act of noticing, of actively observing the land where you live—not from the perspective of someone on the outside looking in, but instead as a part of that same system—that will form much of your work through Ostara. It is this shift in perspective that is key in beginning to link the cycles of the seasons and the rhythms of the natural world to the Wheel of the Year in a way that fosters and develops that animistic worldview.

Throughout the weeks and days leading up to and extending beyond Ostara, you might just be surprised at how active the birds are as they start to mate and collect nesting material. Oftentimes, when we are first beginning to take more notice of our surroundings, birds are perhaps the most notable and easiest animals to watch, particularly for those in more urbanised areas. And one of the things you will begin to notice about them at this time is the dawn chorus.

As you continue to work through this book and forge your own practice, one that is centred around animism and the natural world, you will become familiar with the ebb and flow of the dawn chorus throughout the year. For now though, it is at its peak.

And oh, what a glorious song it is too!

The dawn chorus is unmistakable. It begins with just a solitary voice, usually the blackbird where I live. A few chirps and tweets join the single melody before others add their voices, and before long you have a symphony of melodic springtime beauty, a masterpiece for the ears. Eat your heart out, Vivaldi; this is the real soundtrack of the spring!

In reality, the dawn chorus is communication between birds. The birdsong acts in a number of ways. Sometimes it is in defence of territory (blackbirds are particularly territorial, and you'll often see one male chasing off another), but it is also a mating call, and this is what the dawn chorus is particularly associated with.

I'm lucky that I have quite a large garden, at least in comparison to my neighbours, and as such, I have several mature trees and shrubs. These make great homes for the birds and other creatures that live there.

I have two gardens, one at the front of my home and another at the rear, both connected by a passageway that runs along the side between a wall of ivy that has grown and overtaken the fence. To be fair, it's probably holding the fence up. The ivy is home to a quarrel of sparrows. Sparrows are perhaps one of the most common birds in the UK; they are certainly one which most people will be familiar with. There is nothing particularly special about these greyish-brown little birds. They do not have attractive or eye-catching plumage, nor is their song melodic, and yet despite the ordinariness of this little brown bird, there is something so very charming about them.

Over the course of the years I have spent connecting with the land and the spirits that reside where I do, I have come to adore the sparrows. Their chirpy chatter cannot help but raise the spirits, and their antics in the garden are a delight to behold: the way the young descend like a conquering horde midmorning as they search the garden, plants, and furniture for a morning snack; the way they are such good parents, feeding their young fledglings; how they dominate the fat ball feeder that hangs from the cherry tree. They are the cutest gang! The garden would not be the same without them, and in this way, we can begin to see how important each separate part of nature is. Everything has worth, has merit, and not for what it can give or offer but simply for being exactly what it is. The same applies to us too.

Exercise: Ostara Dancing Meditation

This meditation consists of three parts. The first part is about building on your observations and experiences within your local landscape. In the second part, you'll begin to assimilate your experiences and make correlations to other areas. The final part is the meditation itself.

Part One:

For you and the land where you live, the signs of the season may well be different than the ones I have already discussed. During the first part of this exercise, you will need to go outside. You'll find this is a common theme of the book, spending time in nature, and you'll already have begun on this journey. Making a consistent effort to spend time daily or weekly outside means that you will be better able to observe and experience the subtle changes that occur, that are often overlooked or missed completely. It's this nuance and understanding that will really inform the meditation, making it unique to you and the land where you live.

Try and go at the same time each day. You can make this a part of your morning routine by taking your tea or coffee with you, or by going for a stroll around your garden if you have one. You can do this part as many times as you like, and this can develop into a part of your daily practice if you find it useful. Two or three mornings throughout the week is adequate for this meditation though.

While taking your morning drink outside or going for a walk might seem so mundane, what you are doing is actively choosing to be a part of that moment, a part of that living landscape, and this puts you in a special position from which to watch the morning unfurl in all its glory. Watching and observing can sound like passive activities, and while they certainly can be, they also provide an opportunity to gain a deeper understanding of the land and the routines of the season at that particular time.

Part Two:

Now that you have gotten a feeling of this time of year and at this hour of the day, it's time for the second part of this exercise. Here you'll mull over your experiences and how they impacted you. Did you notice how the day feels as it unfolds? What you can see and hear? How it makes you feel? This is an integral part of any kind of relationship building, but here it will allow you to select an appropriate piece of music for the meditation itself. What constitutes "appropriate music" is absolutely defined by you.

One of my favourite pieces of music for this meditation is "Natural Light" by Ludovico Einaudi. When I listen to this and close my eyes, no matter where I am, I am instantly transported to my garden in the early spring at dawn. I can see the pale golden light that catches the dewdrops in the grass like hundreds of jewels. I can hear the sweet song of the blackbird or robin, the twittering of the sparrows as they awaken in the ivy.

Music bridges the gap between our imagination and our reality in a different way than words or images alone. Music allows us to explore with all of our senses, including our senses of vestibular (balance), propriocep- tive (movement), and interoceptive (internal). This makes using your cho- sen music in this meditation a powerful way of raising the potent energy of Ostara.

Part Three:

Now it's time for the third part, the meditation itself. You can do this inside or outside if you have a safe and comfortable space. Allow your breathing to remain normal and even as you relax into this exercise. At the end of each session, make any notes you feel are necessary in your journal. The gen- eral idea is to begin to bring together your associations and experiences of being in that space at that time with the music you have chosen. This in itself is a beautiful and moving exercise that will strengthen and grow the bonds you have already begun creating.

And now let the dancing commence! Now, I know that the idea of dancing might fill you with dread, but the important thing to remember is that this exercise is for you and you only. This disconnect with our bod- ies is something that so many of us feel at different times of our lives, and this meditation is a good way of reconnecting with our bodies in the same way we have been reconnecting with the land. It's important we view our bodies as a part of the natural world and landscape in much the same way we might view the other beings we share that space with. While it can be hard to work against the conditioning we have experienced about our own bodies (through media, pop culture, bullying, etc.) and there are no quick fixes, this meditation can be an exercise that allows you to work with your body without judgment and shame.

Exercise in particular is a great way of quieting that chattering part of your mind, that voice that provides a constant monologue. For other people, it might be images instead of a voice, or something else, but regardless of what form this "chattering" takes, it all has the same effect of distracting you. And so exercise can not only preoccupy this active part of your mind, it also tires it out as your body tires and becomes focussed on the task. This then leaves those deeper parts of your mind and psyche to connect with the music and your previous experiences to bring about the desired state of mind.

You can choose to play the music as loudly or as quietly as you wish, though do make sure it is loud enough to hear. You might even wish to use headphones to create a more immersive experience. Begin by simply moving to the music in any way you wish. If you are feeling really self-conscious, then try a few "icebreaker" exercises such as planning a sequence of movements or steps, like moving in circles or swinging your arms above your head. Push through any feelings of awkwardness by closing your eyes and bringing to mind your outdoor space. Slowly, you'll ease and unwind into this meditation as you see yourself moving through the garden, inspired by your experiences and the music. Soon, you'll find that you slip easily into meditation while moving to your music.

Losing yourself in an experience such as exercise can be beneficial in many ways, adding to your witchcraft practice. And of course, you should adapt this exercise to suit your own individual circumstances, perhaps by choosing another activity instead of exercise (particularly if you have mobility issues). Repetitive activities like sewing, knitting, and so on can all be beautiful ways of meditating.

Visualisation: Ostara

As with the other visualisations you will encounter in this book, this one is useful whenever you want to evoke the feelings, power, and energy of Ostara, which can be useful before you undertake any spellwork that makes use of those energies. As with the exercise before, the more you begin to connect with nature, the more you will build upon this simple guided meditation, making it more relevant to where you are.

> *Close your eyes.*
> *See yourself in a garden alive with the new shoots of spring.*
> *Hear the dawn chorus all around you.*
> *One of the individual songs seems to stand out from all the others, and you follow this tune. It's melodic and clear, and the other birdsong seems to become but a backing track to this.*
> *Feel the energy of the dawn chorus flow into you.*
> *It inspires hope and wellbeing and just a general feeling of goodness.*
> *Feel these swell within you for as long as you need.*

You can even include your music from the previous meditation for this visualisation. Music has the added benefit of making an activity such as this more accessible, particularly as most people can squeeze in the length of a song into their day at some point.

Beltane (30th April–1st May) ~ May Eve

By the time Beltane rolls around, it's fair to say that spring has well and truly sprung, and not only that, but summer is so close, you can almost feel it. Indeed, we can look at Beltane as something of a liminal celebration, as the line between spring and summer becomes blurred. There is something of a celebratory and joyous air about Beltane; it almost feels like a party. Perhaps it is because summer is almost here and is increasingly at the forefront of our minds as we look forward to holidays, vacations, precious time with family and friends, making memories, and just living our best lives. I think that is definitely part of it, but I also think those feelings of energy and joy we are feeling are a reflection of what is happening to the land and in nature.

Beltane has its origins as a Celtic fire festival that was held throughout the British Isles but is particularly associated with Ireland, Scotland, and the Isle of Man. While there are accounts of the celebration being held in different parts of Britain, this shouldn't be taken to mean there was a uniform celebration, but rather there were independent celebrations that would have differed greatly due to regional variations and customs. What this highlights is that Beltane is and should be firmly rooted in the land and the cycles of nature.

Fire is certainly a major theme of Beltane, and there is some debate as to whether this is shown in the name. Some arguments suggest the celebration takes its name from Bel (other spellings include Bil and Belenos), often associated with fire, and a common practice was lighting fires for purification and protection. On returning their cattle to pasture after the winter months, farmers would drive them between two fires for purification, protection, and luck. People would also jump over or between fires for the same reasons.

Beltane is also associated with May Eve and May Day, which occur at the same time. Today, May Day can be seen through the lens of worker rights, particularly in the UK (May Day, or rather the first Monday in May is a bank holiday when many people have a day of paid leave linked to the International Workers' Day), and rightly so too. However, in Britain, May Eve and May Day are linked to the land and the cycles of nature. We can see this in the custom of "Bringing in the May," whereby people would bring seasonal flowers and foliage into their homes.

Fertility is also an important aspect of Beltane. The Maypole dancing and electing of a May queen can be viewed in terms of sex and fertility. Nowadays, where the tradition continues, we are familiar with the concept of the May queen being a child, but in times past, the May queen would have been a young girl on the cusp of womanhood, and the Maypole is the obvious phallic symbol. However, whereas Ostara regards fertility and sex in terms of procreation and new life, there is a lusty feeling about Beltane and May Eve, and there are lots of references to young men and women "courting" for the night, such as this old country tune:

> *Thus the Robin and the Thrush,*
> *Musicke make in every bush.*
> *While they charme their prety notes,*
> *Young men hurle up maidens cotes.*[4]

As amusing as this verse is, it also points to the link between human feelings and emotions and similar occurrences within the land. The onset of summer and the prospect of easier living, if only for a while, fills everyone with joy—human and beast alike. Life is good right now; everything is growing lush and fertile thanks to the April sunshine and showers; the temperature is warm and rising steadily. The hope that came with the beginning of spring and Ostara is now beginning to blossom and bloom and is on the verge of realisation. We can feel it within ourselves and the land.

Meditation: Beltane

With joyous expectation in the air, Beltane is what I often think of as one of the most exciting sabbats, both in terms of celebrations and energy. We see this in the land, fertile and brimming with life: lambs in the field; green, green grass and foliage; the dusky blue-purple of dog violets; white daisies;

---

4. The original author of this verse is unknown, but it is recorded in various sources; "A Pleasant Countrey Maying Song," English Broadside Ballad Archive, University of California at Santa Barbara, Department of English, c. 1625, https://ebba.english.ucsb.edu/ballad/20010/image.

the pinks of herb Robert; and of course, the white blossom of the hawthorn tree, mayflower.

This time will be different for all of us, no matter where we are. Even for areas that are close in proximity, the microclimates and ecosystems of specific areas can have massive differences in terms of what grows there and when (hence the importance of getting to know the land local to you). This meditation, then, seeks to allow you to explore the energies that are latent in the land where you live and draw on your own experiences.

As mentioned in the "How to Use This Book" section, it may well help to make a recording first. Keep your journal to hand for any notes you wish to make at the end of the meditation, as well as a jumper or blanket in case you get cold partway through. And that's it! You can do this meditation inside or out, but wherever you do, try to minimise any distractions. Get comfortable and we will begin.

Close your eyes and let your breathing come naturally. Allow your body to relax. Just let any thoughts come and go; simply acknowledge them before letting them pass on by.

Notice how relaxed you feel and how those feelings spread through your body, reaching down to the tips of your fingers and toes.

Spend some time now just enjoying those sensations.

When you are ready, take a deep breath and hold it in for a count of four or for however long is comfortable before releasing. Allow your breathing to return to normal.

You are outside your house, perhaps in a garden or your street or a local park. It is sunset, and already the light has taken on that translucent quality. Notice the familiar features of where you are: the birds, trees, plants, and other features that make that space. Feel your spirit reaching out towards them. Feel their own reaching out towards you.

There's an energy in the air, a feeling of excitement. It reminds you of being a little kid at a fairground: anticipation and something else, something more primal, more animal. Natural. A creative urge, but creation for its own sake, for its own pleasure.

As the sunset stretches to twilight and the blackbird and robin sing the last of the day's songs, you begin to move through the space you find yourself in, exploring the familiar and the unknown alike. You can hear the spirits of this land, whispering in excitement as you pass by, feel them reaching out to your own spirit.

Spirit recognises spirit.

Soon you come to a hawthorn tree in bloom. The scent of the flowers hangs in the cool night air, sweet and almost spicy, and they seem to glow in the dark, for night has now fallen.

You brush the blooms and the new leaves with your fingers and place a hand on the trunk. The tree is alive. Can you feel it? Can you extend your consciousness, your spirit out towards the tree and feel it return the effort?

When you feel ready, you quickly make a simple crown using the hawthorn. It is time to Bring in the May, and so, mayflower crown in place, you turn away from the tree and back to your familiar place. You go into your home and into a comfortable place where you light a candle. Soon the sun will rise, but for now, the candle is the only illumination. Lose yourself in the sway of the candle. Feel the energy of the season within you.

Take a deep breath and hold it in for as long as is comfortable before exhaling. Become aware of your body and the sensations within it. Notice any sounds in the room, and when you feel ready, open your eyes. Have a drink of water or a bite to eat, such as a biscuit or sweet to help with the grounding process, and make any notes in your journal about your experiences, thoughts, and feelings.

Exercise: Identifying Plants, Trees, and Animals

So far, I have discussed various ways of beginning to build familiarity and connection to the land, concentrating on the cycles of day and night and of the moon. All of this is so incredibly helpful in gaining those initial connections, but now it is time to go deeper, to take the next step.

Being able to identify animals, plants, and trees is an important skill. It helps in foraging for food and ingredients for your witchcraft practice and will allow you to build your knowledge about what grows where and when, as well as the animals that live in and visit the area. This is one of the best ways of building up your knowledge and understanding of the local landscape.

Identifying the fauna and flora of your local area is something that will take years, but do not be disheartened; that's what makes it so fun! As much of a cliche as it is, the truth is, you will always discover something new. That's the beauty of nature. And you can start anytime. However, at Beltane almost everything has started to grow again, and there will be plenty of hints available to help you identify specific plants and trees. If you were to start in winter, for example, by then the deciduous trees have lost their leaves, and so you would only have the bark and perhaps height to go on, and that's without considering all the other plants that have died back completely until the spring.

To begin, all you really need is yourself, comfortable clothing, and footwear suitable for the terrain and weather. For the first time, simply go for a walk. Allow yourself plenty of time, as you will be walking slowly, stopping and starting so you can examine, explore, and really take notice of the plants, flowers, and trees. At this stage don't worry about trying to identify them, but do take note of plants and trees that commonly occur. Looking for these patterns can help you get a good head start when it comes to identifying flora, but they can also tell you more about that particular area, which in turn will help when it comes to identifying other plants. For example, if you have identified one plant that grows in full sun in poor soil, this then allows you to narrow your identification parameters, and so any other plants that grow there and are flourishing must also prefer poor soil and full sun.

Books can be a massive help when it comes to identifying plants, trees, flowers, and animals, though there are a few pointers to consider when choosing a suitable one. First and perhaps most obvious, make sure you choose a book that is relevant to the area you live in. There's little point having a book about British plants if you live on the other side of the world. Size is also something you should consider. Ideally you will want a small pocketbook so you can carry it with you on your walks and a larger, more in-depth one you keep at home. A big, heavy book would be tiresome and cumbersome to carry but can give extra information about the item you are trying to identify. Next, and perhaps most important of all, make sure the pictures are detailed. Ideally you will want a book with clear, colour photographs of the plant as well as information regarding height, spread, habitat, when it flowers, and descriptions of flower and leaf shape, size, and arrangement.

Plant apps can be extremely helpful when it comes to the identification of plants and trees, which makes sense. After all, most of us have our phones with us the majority of the time. However, as useful as plant apps are, it's important to still learn how to identify plants and trees by sight. Once you have that knowledge, it will always be with you. In truth, you will probably use a mixture of all of these methods. Why not? I do. It makes sense to use the resources we have at our fingertips, especially when you consider the negative consequences of wrong identification.

The skills you learn will be invaluable in your mundane life but will also be important in your witchcraft practice, both from a practical point of view but also in regard to developing an animistic practice. By knowing what grows and flourishes in your local landscape, you can begin to work with the spirits of those plants and trees and to develop that relationship. In doing so, this feeds into the folklore aspect and in turn helps to build a more complete picture of the interconnectedness of the land and ourselves.

Springtime Fun and Magic

There is a particular energy to spring, one that can feel frenzied, joyous, hopeful, or a mixture of all of them. This makes it a great time to try new things simply for the sheer joy of it. Harnessing whatever feelings and energy you see, sense, and feel in nature at this time and bringing them into your home and life can be a great way of developing a practice that is shaped by your connection to the land. It can also help bridge the gap between simply being in nature and observing it and something deeper, an embodied practice informed by your own lived experiences.

Exercise: Springtime Décor

Our homes are important to us and can extend beyond the physical bounds of our properties to encompass our communities and the land. My home is not just my house, but my street, my wider town, and the very land itself. The connection between all of these things is extremely important, especially in terms of cultivating an animistic witchcraft practice.

Decorating your home and altar with natural and seasonal items is a good way of getting out and about in nature as well as inviting the Beltane energies into your home—a modern-day Bringing in the May!

First though, you will need to make several excursions into your area, and there's no reason why you cannot combine this exercise with the previous one, as it does indeed build on the knowledge gained. Positive identification of plants and trees, even for decorations, is important, especially if you have pets or children in the home. The first excursion might just be a scouting expedition to see what is growing and what can be used. How often you can get out is up to you, but I suggest at least a couple of times, as this will give enough time to gather what you need safely. And over the course of the days, you could visit different areas. One day might be a woodland, the next a field.

Look for fallen twigs and sticks that can be made into wreaths and used to fashion hanging decorations. There should be plenty of foliage around right now too, and collecting a little for vases is an easy way of bringing the outside in, always taking care to cause as little damage as possible to the plant and anything else in the area. Decorate your porch with mayflowers (though you might not want to bring them inside the home because folklore tells us it is bad luck to do so).

There are no right or wrong ways of doing this exercise. Take inspiration from nature and from your own aesthetic tastes to really help you bring Beltane into your home in a way that respects and works with the natural rhythms of that place.

Exercise: Growing Plants

One of the easiest ways of incorporating spirit work and animism into one's own witchcraft practice is to grow and tend plants. By looking after the needs and cares of a plant, by watching it grow and learning about what it likes and what it doesn't, you can build a relationship with the plant spirit. This relationship is something that slowly unfurls and is so subtle you may not even notice it at first, but it will happen. It is also a good way of generally following the seasons too, as the plant will have different care needs at different times of the year.

One way of doing this is by growing a plant from seed. Don't worry, you do not need to be an expert gardener, nor is it a necessity to have access to a garden or yard. There are many options you can consider such as window boxes and inside plants. And there are loads of plants that are easy to grow and care for.

Try growing these plants from seed. Not only are they easy to grow and look after, they each have important uses that can help you connect with the season and begin working with those particular plant spirits:

- *Nasturtium:* These are so easy to grow and look after, you wouldn't believe! Suitable for the garden or for baskets and pots, nasturtium seeds need only be pushed into the soil where you want them to grow. They thrive in poor soil and enjoy full sun, though will tolerate partial shade. They will also attract butterflies and bees. Not only that, the leaves and flowers are edible. The leaves make a tasty addition to salads, and the flowers are a real treat when iced and look beautiful on cakes.
- *Basil:* One of the easiest herbs to grow from seed, basil can be grown inside and out, sown into seed beds or grown in pots. It is a must-have herb in the kitchen, and fresh basil tastes so much better than dried. It also has many applications in witchcraft and can be used to infuse anointing oils, dried for incense, and used in spellwork.

- **Any native wildflower species:** These can often be picked up in premixed packs where a range of wildflower seeds are already mixed in compost. All you need to do is prepare the area you want them to grow by clearing and raking before spreading the mixture evenly and watering. Native wild plants and flowers are particularly helpful when it comes to looking after the land around us and thus building connection to nature. Wildflowers attract a variety of pollinators, which in turn attract larger animals such as birds and small mammals, which in turn attract larger predators. Not only does a wildflower garden look beautiful, it helps create a healthy and balanced ecosystem.

If growing plants from seed just seems a little too much right now, there are plenty of plants you can buy that are ready to simply be placed where you want them. Not only are these plants cheap to buy (most young plants are), but they are also particularly easy to look after, even for plant novices:

- **Spider plant:** A favourite houseplant of mine, spider plants are fast-growing and easy to look after. So-called because of their elongated leaves that grow over the pot, making them look like spider legs, these plants require a bright room away from direct light, though will tolerate shade. The best thing about them, though, is how they produce new plants. A healthy plant, once it reaches maturity, will start throwing off long stems that produce small white flowers. As the flowers die away, a new plant begins to form, anywhere up to three or four per stem. Some people like to leave these grow, and they look good when in hanging pots or planters, but if you wish to gain some new plants, you can simply pinch off a spiderling and push it down into some soil or sit it in a small jar of water and watch as roots develop in a matter of days.
- **Succulents and cacti:** These are really easy to care for, especially if you are a little forgetful when it comes to watering, as they don't require daily attention.

- ◆ *Air plants:* If you really can't commit to a watering schedule, then air plants are for you! They take their moisture from the air (though do require some care, check the label), and there are lots of beautiful hangers and holders to display them in all their glory.
- ◆ *Herbs:* If space is something of an issue, then you can make the most of what you have available by choosing herbs. Many herbs can be grown successfully on a sunny windowsill, and you can pick young plants up cheaply from any market or garden centre. The plus side to having herbs is their versatility; you can then use them in the kitchen as well as in your witchcraft practice too.

Exercise: A Spell to Grow Desire

Spring is quite often associated with rebirth and new growth, and so it makes sense to tap into these energies to manifest what it is you want to achieve for yourself, whatever that is. This spell does indeed harness the power of growth and nature.

For this spell, you will need:

- ◆ A plant pot
- ◆ Compost or soil
- ◆ Seeds of your choice (all of the ones included in the exercise above are very easy to germinate and care for)
- ◆ A white candle
- ◆ Pen and paper

I like to do this spell outside in my garden. Not only does it allow me to connect with the spirits of the land, but it makes it easier to clean up any mess. You can do this spell wherever you feel comfortable, but if you do decide to do it inside, then just be aware it can be messy due to potting soil.

Gather everything you need and light the candle. Spend a few moments in quiet contemplation or meditation. Bring to mind what it is you want to achieve, what it is you want to grow and manifest in your life. Visualise this unfurling like the leaves and petals on a plant or flower. See it growing and opening and giving forth all you wish for yourself. When this is as clear as it can be in your mind's eye, write it on the paper and fold it up. Place to one side.

Now it's time to start filling the pot with soil. When the pot is about a quarter filled, push the paper into the pot and continue to fill the pot with soil. Push the seed into the soil and say:

From the smallest seed, great trees do grow.
From my mind, my dreams I sow.
Watered and sunned with my will and toil,
My dreams manifest, push up from the soil.
Grow strong, unfurl, and bloom.
All I hope will manifest soon!
All I will, come to me.
As I will it, so shall it be!

Spring's Song

As you move through the spring, you'll form your own relationships, reach your own understanding in relation to the land and the spirits. These will move, motivate, and inspire you in a variety of ways, whether that's art, singing, writing, dancing, or taking some meaningful action, either for yourself, your community, or the very land and the spirits themselves. I've found that, quite often, it's all of these things to varying degrees. This is my spring song, an ode to the spirits of the land and of spring.

In like a lion, out like a lamb,
Or so the saying says.
Spring is here, as I am
To honour the old ways.
Life is stirring, slowly waking
Dark and cold as the season begins

Like the dawn as day is breaking,
Yet in the dark, the bird still sings
Calling in the first spring day.
In like a lion, out like a lamb,
Or so the saying says.
Spring is here, as I am
To honour the old ways.

Chapter 7
Songs of Summer

◆◆◆◆◆◆

As surely as night follows day, the wheel trundles on, and spring gives way to summer, that glorious season many seem to look forward to. Vacations and holidays, either at home or abroad, those long school breaks—those are what the summer brings to mind. Warmer weather makes the cold of winter feel like some half-remembered dream. In the agricultural calendar of Britain and Europe, it is a time of maintenance and, later on, the hard work of the harvest, which is reflected in the sabbats of the season: Litha, otherwise known as Midsummer, and Lughnasadh, sometimes called Lammas. But there's more to the season and the sabbats than agricultural events many feel disconnected from. The energies that abound in nature at this time do so in us to varying degrees. Throughout spring, you've been on a journey of discovery, both of the land and yourself. As the wheel has turned, passing through Ostara and Beltane, you have started building a relationship with the land where you live and the genius loci there, whether you realise it or not. From the very first time you went out with the intention of consciously observing, feeling, and participating in the natural world around you, you began to build a deep and meaningful connection. And now as the wheel comes to Litha and Lughnasadh, it is time to take stock of the journey so far.

The sun reveals all, and if you want clarity, the summer sun can give you that. By taking the time to look back on your journey, you'll see just how far you have come, how much progress you have made, how much you have learned. And by recognising all of this, by acknowledging this beginning, it will put you in good stead to continue this connection. This type of active remembering goes deeper than just looking at your journey through the year so far. It can extend back to those earliest memories. You might be surprised at what you can recall when you start!

I've always thought children are most wild in the summer months. I know my sisters and I were. Even now, if I close my eyes and think back to our childhood summers, I can't help but smile at all the things we got up to. We were so carefree, felt so brave. As a parent myself, I can't help but wince at some of our adventures, but back then it was different. Times change I guess, and with them, what is considered acceptable.

From the age of around thirteen or fourteen, my oldest sister was often left to babysit us while our parents went out to work. Quite a normal practice back then. But alas, what teenager wants to stay in the house on those hot summer days, stuck with their siblings? None of them! And so, much to the delight of us younger siblings, wherever she went with her friends, we trailed behind. Don't feel too bad for her though. Her friends were all in the same boat, meaning there would be loads of us estate kids. And oh, what fun we had!

We would often go to the woods. This small woodland was about a ten-minute walk from our home across the industrial estate and a field. "Devil's Woods," the locals called it. I have no idea whether that is the real name or not, but the locals still call it that today. Quite often we'd play in the old air raid shelter there, the older kids using lighters to make fire or create a strobe light effect. It always reminded me of those old-fashioned light boxes used to make drawings come to life in staccato stop-start motions.

It didn't take long for us younger kids to get bored listening to the gossip of the older teens and so, no doubt much to their relief, we'd take ourselves off to the woods for more exciting adventures.

Those gloriously golden days of summer were filled with delight and special places, and each holds a memory to be treasured forever. A particular favourite was newt and toad catching along an abandoned railway line. It's still there but has been transformed, made into a cycle track, one of the better schemes that has worked for both nature and humans.

We'd also go to the river, another of those places that seems to provide a backdrop to these summer memories, so often did we visit the riverbank. The boys from the estate would jump off the elbow bridge into the water below, a feat I was far too terrified to try.

And I remember the field, where every summer travellers would pitch up in their caravans and we'd make friends with the kids. Now, whenever I look back through the tumble of my childhood memories, nature was always there.

Now, as an adult with my own children, I have revisited those places and shared the magic of my youth with my children and seen the delight of their own discoveries. My hope is to encourage the closeness to nature that enhanced my childhood and made it something special.

Nowadays, though, there is no swimming in the river because this particular stretch is commercial, running through the centre of the town. And yet, every summer there are those rebellious teens who will make the swim and the front of the local paper. Perhaps that sense of exploration, of immortality, and the feeling of youth and longevity, of the every essence of summer, stirs something inside of them.

It's not just human young who enjoy the summer sun. You can see it yourself: Young sparrows are a delight to watch as they play, bold and bolshy and so very cute, even as they squabble for the tastiest of my young pea shoots. Fox cubs, glimpsed in the long grasses of the riverbank, leap and roll and play fight under the watchful gaze of their mother in the evening sun. Solar energy is strong and potent. It fills many of us with energy and joy in varied ways, just as it does the land around us and the other beings we share this world with.

Litha (21st–22nd June) ~ Midsummer ~ The Summer Solstice

Litha marks the longest day of the year and, of course, the shortest night. After this moment, the days will gradually get shorter, the nights longer, but for now, this is summer—Midsummer at that. The earth is at the most northerly point of its orbit, and so the sun appears higher in the sky, and we in the Northern Hemisphere get more sunlight.

Midsummer feels gauzy, like a dream. The wheel has turned, and the lusty energy of Beltane has been spent. Now it's time for long and luxuriant pleasure to be stretched out and enjoyed to its fullest extent, every last drop to be consumed and enjoyed, and we can see this mirrored in nature too.

In terms of the agricultural year on which the Wheel of the Year is based, there is nothing much to do besides maintenance work. The crops have already been sown and are growing, and it is not yet time for the harvest. The first of the year's chicks have fledged, and some species will be on their second or even third clutch of eggs already. For other animals, the young are already born or soon to be. Flowers and grasses are flowering and seeding, providing bountiful food for the wildlife.

Life generally feels good.

Midsummer is very much about taking the time to appreciate these things and enjoying this moment. The longest day seems to put everything into perspective. Perhaps the beauty and almost dream-like quality of Midsummer is made even more beautiful because the moment is fleeting, and on some level, we and the creatures we share our world with know this. Nothing lasts forever as it is; all exists within the cycles of nature. Life and death go hand in hand—abundance and scarcity. But for now, it is enough to simply stop and enjoy the beauty of a midsummer's day, to enjoy this time of happiness and easy living before the toils of the harvest and the prospect of darker and colder weather becomes a reality.

Recently, I spent the solstice in the woods with my group, and true to form, it was a cloudy and somewhat cool sunset beneath the boughs, but it didn't matter. Listening to the breeze through the leaves and the sway of the trees, the call of wood pigeons and the chatter of magpies, feeling the forest floor beneath me—this is what it's all about, what makes the sabbat important. It doesn't matter that we didn't see the sun. We are a part of nature and the cycles of it. Making time to just enjoy nature without reason, simply for the sake of enjoying it, is the essence of Litha.

It can often be hard for us to do "nothing," especially those of us who live in Western industrialised nations, because we very rarely do nothing. The reasons for this are varied. Often, we don't have the time or are tired. When we do make that extra effort or find time, then it can sometimes feel like we have to catch up with other stuff. It can feel odd to just go outside for the sake of going outside, to just enjoy the sensations of the earth and the sun and everything in between, but it is needed. Not everything spirit-work related has to be about "doing" something. In spending some quiet time alone out-side at this, the height of summer, we can often hear and feel the spirits the most.

At the summer solstice, the longest day, it is important we give ourselves some time and space to just enjoy being at one with the world around us, and the exercises you find in this section can help with that.

Meditation: Litha

Some of the most common reasons people give for not being able to meditate effectively include not being able to sit still for long enough, lack of time, and being unable to quiet their mind. These are all genuine reasons, and I know I have struggled with them in the past; however, they can be overcome, and Litha is a great time to try alternative methods of meditation.

We have come to think of meditation as this thing that can only be achieved if you sit or lay in a particular position for long enough, and yet this isn't true. People meditate for many different reasons, and there are just as many different methods to suit these reasons.

A walking meditation is a fantastic way of getting out in midsummer. It is a way of building familiarity and relationship with the land and the genius loci. It can also be a great way of meditating without labouring over it. You will need to find somewhere that is relatively quiet, where you won't be interrupted too much; after all, you don't want to run into someone you know, a friend or acquaintance perhaps, and for them to keep you chattering for a good part of your walk. You can do this meditation at any time of day, though it might be useful to choose a quieter time of the day, such as early morning or in the evening.

To begin, then, simply start walking.

At first it will feel very much like an ordinary walk, and that's absolutely fine—necessary, in fact. It might be a good idea to walk for five minutes at a fast pace, or a faster pace than is normal for you. Not only does this give you a chance to blow away the cobwebs and release any steam or tension, but it also allows you time to acclimatise to being outside. Often when I go for a meditative walk, I need those first five minutes to just get used to being outside, to allow myself to attune and cast off the miasma of the day. Slowly, I stop replaying those instances that have annoyed me throughout the day. This happens all by itself simply by virtue of being out in nature, but you'll know when it has because you will feel lighter, a little more at ease, no matter what else is going on in your life. When you feel that shift, then it's time to begin your meditation.

Do not be mistaken, a walking meditation isn't the same as simply going for a walk and losing yourself. As with any meditation, there is a need for active participation, and so to begin, focus on your breathing. Take a deep breath and then another. What does the air smell of? Allow your breathing to fall into a comfortable rhythm, and as you do, begin to notice, to really see, the plants, trees, birds, and insects around you. If there are flowers, let your gaze hover over them, unfocused so that the colours seem to sway and come alive. Feel the air on your skin. Is it warm or cold? Notice the patterns of the sun, of light and shade. What sounds can you hear, human and beast? Feel your spirit rise and swell inside of you as it responds to the Litha energies.

As you near the end of your walk, take a deep breath and hold for as long as is comfortable before exhaling. Slow your pace and notice any sensations in your body. When you get home, you may wish to do some light stretching if you are able and have a cold drink. Make any notes in your journal.

It would be good form to keep this practice up. Once or twice a week is all you need throughout the season of Litha, and as you begin to familiarise yourself with the land and nature, you'll get a better understanding of anything that comes through or occurs during the meditation.

Exercise: Midsummer Tarot Spread for Clarity

Midsummer is marked by the astronomical event of the summer solstice. This is the longest day. It makes sense to tap into these strong solar energies to gain clarity. In the light of the sun, the light of day, it is easier to see things more clearly as they are and not draped in shadow and mystery. It is this energy the following tarot spread aims to tap into.

You can do this spread wherever you feel comfortable.

Begin by spending a few moments in meditation. You might wish to try the sun visualisation exercise in chapter 4. When you are ready, shuffle your cards, and as you begin to lay them out (as shown below), say aloud, "Show me what I need to see."

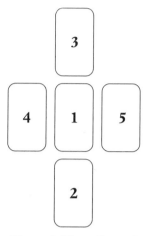

Figure 3: Tarot Spread

1. ***You now:*** This card provides a snapshot of you in the moment. It can highlight your general feelings and emotions at this time.

2. ***Foundation card:*** Our foundations—including where we come from, our families, our own core personalities—influence us more than we may care to realise. This card reminds us we can draw strength from our foundations if we can view them clearly, detached from the emotional baggage that might come with them.

3. ***Head space:*** Our minds are powerful things, and this card relates to our own thoughts and feelings. We all have that inner voice that guides us, that constant monologue, but it can also hinder as much as help. This card lets us see through our own self-doubts and fears.

4. ***The past:*** Good and bad, our experiences help shape our present and future selves. This card highlights a lesson from the past that must still be learned or let go of.

5. ***Something that helps:*** This might be a strength you have and need to draw on, or it might be an action to take. This card highlights something that will help you at least get started towards where you want to be.

Exercise: Active Remembering

Our minds are slippery things. When we think about the act of remembering, it's easy to focus on the long ago, the past, but remembering is an active process. Yes, it is indeed about recalling the things, people, and events that came before, but it is also about considering those memories in relation to the present moment. In this way, it becomes something more than simply remembering the good times and the bad. It becomes a way of assimilating your experiences.

This exercise, then, is about going back out to the area you have been working to develop a connection with, this time viewing it through the lens of your experiences. Pay attention to how the landscape has changed throughout the passing weeks, from the spring and to the summer.

Sketch, draw, paint, or take photographs of your favourite areas. Try and capture what it is that draws you to that space. You might find it useful to keep a thinking diary, different from your journal, where perhaps you can keep mementos of your experiences with the local landscape, such as dried flowers, or where you can sketch or write anything that comes to mind, even if it makes no sense.

This type of active remembering while simultaneously experiencing the land in the present is so very valuable when it comes to furthering your relationship with the land. It allows you the time and space to take stock of all you have achieved while also recognising that this journey is one that is ever ongoing.

Recognising the Needs of Land and Spirit

The land and nature give us so much, from the food we eat to the water we drink and everything else in between. And it's not just the physical benefits either; indeed, many studies show that spending time in nature can help improve mood and emotions, and it's something I have discovered myself through my own experiences with the land.[5] There have been many times when going through hard situations that immersing myself in nature has helped. It sounds awfully romantic, don't you think? But as romantic—or silly, for that matter—as it may well sound, it is actually true. You go out for a walk, and you feel yourself growing lighter. It's like nature puts a buffer between yourself and your problems, and while your issues will still be there when you return, you'll be in a much better frame of mind to begin tackling them in a considered and nuanced way.

Fantastic, right?

It is massive what the land, what nature, does for us, but this then begs the question, what are we doing in return? All relationships require effort from all involved parties; that's how they work. Look back on friendships and other relationships where you've felt the other person doesn't put the same effort in as you. It doesn't feel good, and it's only a matter of time before you drift apart or the relationship disintegrates altogether. It's the same when it comes to building and maintaining relationships with the land and the genius loci. It cannot be a one-way thing; it just doesn't work. In all healthy relationships, there is a giving and a taking, and you will need to ensure you remember this balance.

In terms of witchcraft, this might look like taking into consideration the tools you use and how they are sourced and made. When it comes to spirit work, it could be making sure your offerings are suitable and do not pollute or damage the environment. These are very easy things to do. Instead of leaving plastic or resin statues as

5. "Nature: How Connecting with Nature Benefits Our Mental Health," Mental Health Foundation, 2021, https://www.mentalhealth.org.uk/sites/default/files/2022-06/MHAW21-Nature-research-report.pdf.

offerings, you might instead leave birdseed or flowers. It might mean leaving the beautiful crystal in the shop and instead decorating your altar with stones found in the garden or other natural items.

However, we also need to make sure we follow through in the other areas of our life too. This is what it is to be animist. We see and feel the spirit within the natural world and know we are not separate from it at all, but connected to it in every way. Just as it is hard to separate the many different aspects that make us *us*, nor can we completely separate the mundane, the magical, and the spiritual parts of ourselves. If we hope to build a strong relationship with nature spirits, we need to ground that practice in taking care of nature in the mundane and magical spheres as well.

Taking care of the environment is a good way of getting outside within that environment and can form a part of your relationship building. Try taking a bag for rubbish when you go out in your area on walks and picking up any litter you find. Make the best choices you can when it comes to living a little greener too. There will obviously be compromises you need to make based on your own individual needs, and this might take some time, but the important thing is that you start, no matter how small. In fact, starting small is perhaps the best way to ensure the changes are manageable and long lasting. You'll find that as you begin to really build bonds with the land and nature, you will want to protect it in any way that you can. It's something that happens naturally over time.

Litha is a good time for considering these issues. Make use of the strong solar energies of Midsummer and begin to think about the ways in which you can give back to nature. Don't be afraid to think outside of the box. It might help to make a mind map or list in your journal and start putting together a plan. Act on it. It will not take long for you to begin to see your efforts in the deepening of your relationship with the genius loci.

Lughnasadh (1st–2nd August)

Golden fields of wheat and azure skies. Sunflowers and lavender. When I close my eyes and think of Lughnasadh, this is what I see, feel, and smell. Lughnasadh is hot, the dog days of summer. While the summer solstice is indeed the longest day, it doesn't mean it is the hottest, at least where I live. No, the hottest time of year is August. It also signifies the long, hot summer of youth.

When we were kids, we'd go swimming. The blessed coolness of the river was such a welcome relief. Like I said earlier, most times we went during the heat of day, and not far—a short walk and a level crossing and then you were there. Other times, we'd go further. Much more exciting than the river was the concrete barge.

The river that runs through my town splits into two parts, the old and the new. Back when the town was built, work on the river redirected the water in the form of man-made canals to allow goods to be traded and exported easily. Where the canal and the original river rejoin just outside of the town, there's a lake. On the bank sits an old abandoned concrete barge.

I think I enjoyed the journey there and back the best. It was just so exciting because there was always a crowd of us. I'd often imagine myself in a group not unlike the Famous Five, off on some adventure. The concrete barge was a two-mile walk from where we lived and took us through the next village. Back then it felt much longer, like I was in the 1986 film *Stand by Me*, sans dead body of course!

Concrete barges were used during and after the Second World War but eventually fell out of usage. This one sat on a sandy bank, and though it was collapsed in the centre, it was still sturdy and safe enough if you kept to the outer edges. After clambering up onto the deck, we'd sit there in the hot sun, relishing the feel of warm concrete on bare skin. Some of the older kids would jump off into the cold water, but I was always scared and never the strongest or most confident of swimmers. Once though, I did jump off, but it took a lot of cajoling and promising to catch me from one of the older boys, a teenager the same age as my sister. Props to him—he did catch me, but not before my head went under and I swallowed a mouthful of the water. Then his hands were under my arms, and I was out, the tang of the cold water in my mouth and the hot sun on my skin. I never did dare jump from the concrete barge again, but oh, how I loved those days.

The Harvest

Lughnasadh is the first harvest, and when we grow out of the childish pleasures of the long, hot summer, the work must begin again. That last summer is tinged with happiness and sadness. The last of unbridled youth, all the sweeter because it is indeed the last.

The midsummer was a carefree time, but now the first harvest must be reaped and gathered. There is an excitement about the first harvest, and across the British Isles there are many local and national traditions steeped in folklore associated with this time, such as hand cutting the last of the wheat. Throughout Europe there are traditions such as saving the last cut of corn because the spirit of the corn resides within. It must be brought in and kept safe throughout the winter months before being released the following spring, thus ensuring the continued fertility of the land. Sometimes, this last cut of corn might be crafted into a human shape. These corn dollies represent the Corn Mother, a spirit of the harvest, and there are some wonderful designs out there. Anyone interested in corn dollies and the spirits of the harvest would do well to check out the work of natural fibre artist Victoria Musson. (I had the pleasure of attending one of her workshops; it was simply fabulous.)

Along with Mabon and Samhain, Lughnasadh is one of the sabbats when we are most aware of the spirits of the land. Perhaps this is because we are just beginning to reap the benefits of the harvest, and this reminder of our dependence on the land and our part within nature makes us more aware of spirit. We see this in the continuation of practices such as weaving grain stems and other crafts, songs, and rituals associated with the harvest.

With the harvest, we are also reminded about the cycles of life, death, and nature, and this also adds to the feeling of being closer to spirit at this time. When we reap, we cut down, we kill, and this is highlighted in the story of "John Barleycorn," an old country rhyme, though the most well-known version was written by the Scottish poet and writer Robert Burns. It goes like this:

> *There was three kings into the east,*
> *Three kings both great and high,*
> *And they hae sworn a solemn oath*
> *John Barleycorn should die.*
>
> *They took a plough and plough'd him down,*
> *Put clods upon his head,*
> *And they hae sworn a solemn oath*
> *John Barleycorn was dead....*
>
> *And they hae taen his very heart's blood,*
> *And drank it round and round;*
> *And still the more and more they drank,*
> *Their joy did more abound.*
>
> *John Barleycorn was a hero bold,*
> *Of noble enterprise;*

For if you do but taste his blood,
'Twill make your courage rise.

'Twill make a man forget his woe;
'Twill heighten all his joy;
'Twill make the widow's heart to sing,
Tho' the tear were in her eye.

Then let us toast John Barleycorn,
Each man a glass in hand;
And may his great posterity
Ne'er fail in old Scotland![6]

This poem, sometimes sung as a folk song, is pretty dark, wouldn't you agree? It highlights the closeness, indeed the direct link, between life and death. It also draws attention to the processes involved in making food and drink we might often take for granted. This is the ultimate result of the relationship between ourselves, the land, and the genius loci: survival.

Exercise: A Lughnasadh Journey

Guided meditations and journeying are similar but have some important differences that distinguish them from one another. Guided meditations, such as the ones included in this book, are a good way of helping you enter a state of deep relaxation. They can help to focus that part of your mind that is constantly chattering and looking for distraction. Journeying, on the other hand, has a specific purpose besides just relaxation and concentrating the mind. Any journey requires a beginning and an ending, and this is perhaps one of the most apt ways of describing what a journey hopes to achieve.

6. Robert Burns, "John Barlycorn: A Ballad," in *Poems and Songs of Robert Burns*, Project Gutenberg, accessed June 19, 2023, https://www.gutenberg.org /files/1279/1279-h/1279-h.htm#link2H_4_0031.

Sometimes we might undertake journey work to learn something about ourselves, to connect and commune with spirit, or to bring something back with us, whether this is understanding or new insight. Journeying is a natural next step after meditation.

As with the meditations included throughout this book, you may wish to record yourself reading it aloud first. However, if you are confident at meditating and have mastered the art of redirecting your mind, you may wish to have a go at a more organic journey. You can do this by reading the journey below a few times, and if you can recall each stage of the journey enough so that you can remember the main points, then have a go. Whereas a meditation is very descriptive and leads you, a journey is somewhat different. Though there may be some initial scene setting, the idea is that the journey will tell its own story, unfolding as is needed to reveal the answers or truths you are looking for.

If you wish, you can bathe or shower before the journey, though this is not necessary. Washing your face and hands is enough. Wear loose-fitting or comfortable clothes and keep a blanket close by in case you get cold. Minimise any distractions and we'll begin.

Close your eyes and just spend a few moments allowing your body to relax and acclimatise to your surroundings. Let your breathing come naturally.

You are calm.

You are relaxed.

You are safe.

You are outside. The day is hot, and the sun is high in a cornflower-blue sky. You are standing at the edge of a field of golden wheat. It stretches as far as the eye can see, and there seems to be a path leading into the field, as though someone has walked there before. It draws you forward, a physical force that seems to tug at something in the very core of your being.

You enter the field and follow the path.

Where does it lead you?

Are there twists and turns?

What can you see, hear, smell?

Soon you reach a clearing and standing in the centre of that clearing, her back to you, stands a woman. She wears a dress of gold, bright as the sun, with long golden hair.

She turns to you and holds your hand in hers. She leads you on and on ...

Watch and listen carefully to what she shows you, to what she has to say. Allow yourself to be led by her. Open yourself to her ...

When she has told you all you are ready for, she leads you back to the clearing. You follow the path back to the road. You do not look back.

Slowly become aware of your body, of your breathing. Slowly become aware of the room around you. When you are ready, open your eyes.

Have a drink and something to eat to help with the grounding process before making notes in your journal. It's important you spend some time really exploring the themes and messages of your journey because, as with most things occult, any meaning is often coded in symbolism and imagery and so is not straightforward when it comes to drawing any conclusions.

Consider how you felt during the journey and how these feelings changed throughout, if they even did at all. Also consider colours, people and animals, landscapes, plants, and general feeling, air, or aura. It's also important to pay attention to any dreams you feel might be associated with the journey. With this kind of work, it can take a while for any meaning to become clearer, so don't be too worried if nothing occurs straight away.

Exercise: Making a Corn Dolly

You will need a few ears of wheat with the stems still attached to make your corn dolly, and you may need to check where you can buy this locally. Local florists might be a good port of call, but if you don't want to use corn, there are other options. Perhaps using wheat doesn't feel right for the land where you live. Instead, you can use foliage found in your local landscape as a way of honouring the genius loci. Choose foliage with longer, thicker stems, or perhaps foliage from soft fruit trees.

The corn dolly represents the Corn Mother, the fertile spirit of the harvest, and by making a corn dolly, you are giving this spirit somewhere safe to overwinter before releasing her back to the fields during Ostara.

At the very least, you will need:

- Three ears of wheat with the stems still attached (You can use more wheat if you wish, but you will need at least three. Top tip: odd numbers work better than even!)
- Scissors
- Natural fibre string such as hemp or cotton

I find it useful to cut several lengths of string to begin with. They need to be around 10 cm long. Put them to one side and take up your wheat. The ears will form the head of the corn dolly. Arrange them so that you are happy with how they look and secure together using a piece of string. Take another piece of string and tie the stems together about an inch below the first knotted string. This will form part of the body and will also be where the arms will slide through.

Figure 4: Corn (Wheat) Dolly

Next, take the scissors and carefully trim the stems. You might want to leave a longer stem so that they resemble a dress, or you may wish to shape them using extra string. You can do this by tying and binding the stems together or separating into bundles. There is no right or wrong way, so let your own tastes shape the form. Take the offcuts and bundle them together. Tie each end with a piece of string and neaten up the ends if they require it. Carefully push the bundle through the body of the corn dolly between the first and second pieces of string and adjust until even and so that it resembles arms. You may wish to decorate your corn dolly with dried flowers. Do make sure you use biodegradable materials so that when it comes time to release the spirit back into the fields, everything will break down naturally.

You can keep the corn dolly on your altar if you have one. If you don't, then anywhere safe will be fine. Feed her regularly with offerings of water, incense smoke, and honeyed milk.

Summer and the Fruit Harvest

While apples and pears ripen a little later on, there are many soft fruits that are beginning to ripen at this time. Foraging for fruits such as blackberries, cherries, and elderberries is a fantastic way of connecting to the cycles of the season. Even if you live in more urban areas, there will be parks and other places where you can forage safely.

I have always found foraging to have many benefits, not least fresh food. It helps build that connection and familiarity with the land where you live but also allows you to reconnect the sabbats with the Wheel of the Year.

The estate where I live is dotted with many fruit trees. There are cherry, green and yellow gage, several varieties of plum, sloes, rosehips, and more, and for the most part, people just don't notice. And when they do see me taking a few for the fruit bowl, they often give me a funny look, wondering what that weird woman is up to, before plucking up the courage to ask. And when I tell them, more often than not, they take a few too!

For the most part, particularly with those who live in urban areas, there is a general disconnect with the land. How can the harvest and the agricultural holidays centred around it be relevant when we are so distant from them? I also think that most people simply do not notice what is growing around them or are unable to identify plants and fruits.

The experiences you have gained from spring and throughout summer develop into knowledge. This knowledge combined with and enriched by your experiences will help you when it comes to identifying what is good to eat. The first step is to simply go out. It might be for a look in your garden, street, or neighbourhood before expanding outwards into your wider area. The first outing will act as a sort of scouting trip where you are just looking. If you do notice any fruits growing on trees, then you will need to examine them to get a positive ID. What do they look like? What colour and shape are they? Does the tree or bush have thorns or any other noticeable features? If you have your phone with you, take several pictures to make comparisons, and when you get home, use the internet or books. If you are in any online foraging groups, they can also be very helpful. You could try posting the pictures there.

When you are positive about an identification, next it is important to consider where the fruit is growing. Avoid fruits that grow by roadsides or near industrial sites, as pollutants can be absorbed by the plant and thus enter into the fruits. It's also important to consider whether the area is treated with pesticides. If you are unsure, then don't take the risk. Here is where your familiarity with the local land will help you make informed choices.

If you are sure of identification and the safety of the food to eat, and if it is plentiful, then take some of the fruits. But if the fruit trees are on someone's property, you will need to get permission. In my own experiences, though, most folks are quite happy to share a little of their bounty, and offering to gather some for them while taking a few for yourself can be a good way of building community with your human neighbours! Eat them fresh straight from the tree or take them home and use them in cooking. There is so much you can make with your foraged finds, such as crumbles, cakes and tarts, jams, chutneys, and wines. You'll never be short of ideas.

However, as we have been discovering, the connection to the land is a reciprocal one, and so it is important we honour this and the fruit harvest. You might wish to do this by pouring a libation or leaving an offering of water or seeds for the birds.

Summer's Song

The summer months and sabbats can seem almost romantic or idyllic, so much do they seem to offer, but they are more than that. The land and nature provide so much, but this is a reciprocal relationship, one that requires us to interact with nature and the land. We are not passive bystanders but instead are active, constituent parts of that whole. My season song for the summer plays on this reciprocal relationship but also hints of the magic of the season, when the past and present collide in a multisensory experience that delights.

The sun skims the horizon, breaking free and rising,
Lighting the earth in its golden glow.
The sky is a show, all hues of blue,
Pale deepening to cornflower
And insects sing in the long grasses.
Time lasts for eternity,
The air syrup thick.

I close my eyes and take a deep breath,
Its scent hot, like ironed linen
And carries the perfume of unseen blooms,
Yellows and reds, pinks and purples.
And with it all, they come unbidden,
Like images on my closed lids,
Memories made, forgotten, remembered,
No doubt to be forgotten again.
The hazy beauty of summer days,
The pleasure of its short nights.
But best of all
The grass between my toes.
Or sand.[7]

7. Emma Kathryn, "Songs of Summer," A Beautiful Resistance, Ritona, June 24, 2022, https://abeautifulresistance.org/site/2022/6/24/songs-of-summer.

Chapter 8
Songs of Autumn

◆◆◆◆◆◆

When the cool, damp wind swirls through the boughs and makes the leaves, already turning shades of yellow and orange, shiver and fall, it carries the scent of sugar beet to my nose, and I know autumn has arrived.

There's a big sugar beet factory on the outskirts of the town where I live, and every autumn, when sugar beet is in, processing begins. The smell is deep and earthy. It is one of those things that reminds me of autumn. Strange, you might well think, that someone talking about animism, connection to the land, and witchcraft would be reminded of autumn by a factory. The truth is, though, as a rural town surrounded by farms and countryside, it's instances such as this—the culmination of our relationship with the land and how it supports us—that do mark the seasons and cycles of nature.

Autumn is my favourite season, always has been. While all the seasons indeed hold a magic of their own, my heart belongs to the encroaching gloom and gathering dark of autumn. There is something so deeply soothing in the slowing and settling down, in the retreat—a coming home, if you will.

And yet, despite the connotations of death and darkness, or perhaps in spite of them, there is a spectacular beauty to the season, a beauty that aches with the slow and decadent decay. The trees provide a spectacular colour show more beautiful to behold than any firework or illumination that humans can produce. The murmuration of the starlings is something I love to see and is truly a sight to behold, It's a particular favourite and far more enthralling than any special effect conjured in a Hollywood studio.

The woods are one of my favourite places to be in autumn. I love those bright days when the sun shines golden and hazy, and the wind blows warm but with an edge when the sun disappears behind a cloud. There's just something so special when the leaves turn golden, red, and orange, and oh they fall and cascade when the wind rattles the boughs. The earthy scent of the forest floor and the sweet smell of decay, I love everything about it. But it's not only the beginning of autumn I like, but those dark and damp days too.

If I close my eyes now, I can almost imagine I am there in the woods—can feel my soul beginning to stir, drawing the energy of that place to me, into me. I know that place and the spirits there. It is familiar, and now at this time, I feel them more keenly. Spring might well be the season when life begins to return and grow, but there is a complexity to autumn. It is a melancholic swan song and a grand farewell spectacle: see you next time!

Endings and Beginnings

For many beginners as they start their journey into animism, autumn is often the best time to begin to forge a relationship with the land and the genius loci, as the feeling of transition can be felt so strongly. Children begin settling into the new academic year, and the focus is on change: change of class, sometimes change of friendship groups, new endings, and new beginnings. This transition also occurs in nature. The autumn is full of departures and arrivals as birds begin to migrate. The swifts and swallows that once built nests in the stables at my workplace, who swooped low across river and field in their hunt for winged insects, are gone. The nights are noticeably longer and cooler, even on those still-warm days. As the changes that occur in nature are so dazzling at autumn, it is perhaps easier to feel that connection to the spirit of the season.

Exercise: Morning Sitting Ritual

Like spring, autumn is a time of transition. Changes happen so quickly, it can feel like summer one day and the onset of winter the next, at least in my part of the world. It is an exciting time, and one where the changes that are occurring assault all the senses.

This exercise is one to do every day. It sounds like a lot, but it really isn't; you'll see. And it's so easy too. All you have to do is take your morning drink outside. That's it. Slip on some thick socks and your slippers (or shoes if you'd prefer), wrap a blanket about yourself or pull on a jumper or robe. Sit or stand on your doorstep, or by an open window if you don't have a secure outside space, and simply drink your drink. That's it! Sounds simple, right? And it is, but it is also one of those exercises that has so many benefits.

First of all, it is a great way to start your day. And if you are worried you do not have enough time to do it, then set your alarm for ten minutes earlier than normal, five if you are really squeezed for time. The more you get into the habit of setting time aside for yourself, you'll begin to see the benefit not only for yourself but for those you share your space and life with too.

Not only can this be an important aspect of self-care, the act of simply allowing yourself to *be*, experiencing the moment as it unfolds, this exercise is a good way of building a practice with the emphasis on actually practising. It can be difficult for beginner witches and more seasoned spellcasters to keep a regular practice. Sometimes we just don't know where to begin, and other times it might feel as though we are stuck in a bit of a rut. Sitting outside enjoying your morning beverage may not sound like much of a practice, but it is. Consider the act of sitting quietly as a practice of allowing your body to just be, with no expectations on it at all. Over time, this act of sitting becomes a ritual in and of itself, particularly as you begin to see and feel the benefits of it.

Not only can sitting become a part of your practice in a ritual way, it also serves another purpose, and this is perhaps the aim here. The act of sitting outside is an act of immersion. You are becoming a part of that landscape, of that place. You aren't separate from it but are instead an active, living participant. And what's more, by sitting quietly and watching, you'll begin to get a feel for the changes that are occurring over the course of the season.

You can do this activity at any time, but by starting out at Mabon and finishing after Samhain, it can really be an eye-opener in terms of how much the land and the animals change in such a short time. Perhaps the biggest surprise is how much of it you will see and notice simply by sitting quietly for five to ten minutes a day.

Mabon (21st–22nd September) ~ The Autumn Equinox

Mabon arrives as a break in this cycle of transformation and transition that is autumn. It is the autumn equinox, and like its springtime counterpart, this too is a time of balance. Day and night are of equal length as the sun is directly above the equator.

Although this sabbat marks the autumn equinox and the second harvest, the name Mabon is taken from Welsh lore, most notably the fourteenth-century manuscript called The Mabinogion. Mabon ap Modron is a god figure, son of Modron. The name, however, was only first adopted for the equinox in the 1970s. At this time of year, the weather is changeable. Some days carry a hint of the summer passed while others are windswept and wet. But even with the still-warm days, the air is tinged with the scent of autumn, and the sun sits lower in the sky, even at noon.

This is also the time when there is work to be done in the fields, though today with the advance of technology, it looks very different from the historical harvest, when much of the work was done by hand and involved many people from the local community. This is the harvest proper, a bountiful time when food is plenty. The last of the grains are harvested, as are the root vegetables, sweetcorn, and beans. Apples and pears are ripe and ready to be picked. Blackberries can still be picked right up to the twenty-ninth of the month. There's a piece of folklore that tells us that after this date, the devil either urinates or spits on them, thus rendering them inedible. I love folklore, as it often contains truths that have been passed down through the generations that show our relationship to the land. In truth, by the time we get to the end of September, the fruits of the bramble are old and past their best, too "jammy" even for jam making.

As well as being the equinox, Mabon is also a celebration of the harvest. And this is one of those times when we can see the disconnect between the Wheel of the Year and the lived experiences of many people. I have seen quite a few witches, Pagans, and occultists say they feel very little connection to Mabon as a sabbat. While they may celebrate the date because of the astronomical goings-on, they feel little connection to this part of the season. In part, this harkens back to the loss of connection to the land. While we still and always will rely on the land for our food, our modern way of life has separated most of us from the agricultural year and food growth and production.

Mabon reminds me of being a child again and the harvest festivals that used to be such a big deal but seem to have fallen out of favour in our modern times.

I can remember the first time I made bread from scratch. It wasn't at home, nor was it at the expected time of Lughnasadh, and I wish I could recall some rose-tinted memory of being taught by a beloved granny, but I can't. Instead, it was at primary school, and we were making bread for the harvest festival. Not just any bread, mind, but a plaited loaf. My ten-year-old self thought this the height of sophistication.

I can remember being surprised that the room smelled ever so slightly of beer. Every child was given a piece of dough that had already been kneaded and proved and was ready to be shaped into the final form. The warm dough felt marvellous in my hands, stretchy and oh so soft. We didn't get to eat the bread. Instead, it joined the collection of tinned goods donated by pupils, a hastily clutched tin of something that had sat for months in the cupboard, no doubt. The school would put on a concert for the old people's care home around the corner, and we'd donate the food to them afterwards.

Back then, as a kid sitting in hot and dusty school halls and having to sing songs by rote, the harvest festival often felt stale, like something done for the sake of it. But now as I write this, looking back on sepia-toned memories with my adult's mind, I like to think a little better of those festivals. As unconnected to the land as they may have felt, and indeed were, they hinted at something else, a need to remember what we take from the land and a thanksgiving for the life the land bestows.

Despite the loss of connection to the farming year for most of us, the signs and energies of the season can also be seen reflected in our own lives. Children and students return to school after the summer holidays, and our thoughts might begin to turn to the financial burden that is Christmas and the festive season. While right now is a time of plenty, we know what is to come. There is hard work to be done before the darkness descends completely.

If you have a garden, then there are lots of jobs that need doing now, and you will already have begun to notice the changes that are occurring in nature right now. If you grow fruit and veg, then you too will be busy harvesting and storing your produce. And it's time to cut back many of the woody shrubs and perennial plants and just have a good tidy up before the weather worsens.

And even if you don't have a garden, you will still notice the changes that are occurring in nature at this time. The nights are cooler, the days too, and this is reflected with changes in our habits. We might start to spend longer indoors, relying more on our modern conveniences. There is no escaping the fact that the wheel has well and truly turned.

Meditation: Autumn Equinox

The autumn equinox is a time of balance. At the spring equinox, there was a hopeful and expectant air to this momentary pause, like the moment before a firework blooms with an explosion of sound and colour. This time, there is a more melancholic air. There is a feeling of winding down. This pause is a moment of calm amid the hard graft of the harvest. It is a look back on the easier, more laid-back months of the summer. The balance of light and dark echoes the balance of looking back at our hard work while preparing for the slower times ahead. In this moment of balance, all feels plentiful and yet we know the leaner months will follow.

This meditation aims to home in on these energies. There is a need to look back, to reflect on and even to just enjoy those memories. They have led to this place, to this moment, and we can learn a lot from them in terms of how our relationship to the land has progressed. At the same time, we must look forward and prepare, while also taking the time to just enjoy this moment of balance, of calm amid the transformative energies of Mabon.

As with any meditation, wear comfortable clothing and keep a blanket handy in case you get cold partway through. Minimise distractions and get into a comfortable position before closing your eyes.

Spend a few moments just concentrating on your breathing. Allow each breath to come naturally. Allow yourself to notice any noises inside and outside of the room. Notice how relaxed you begin to feel. Feel it spread through you, perhaps in pulses or maybe waves or even just a soft creeping. Notice how relaxed you feel. Take a deep breath in through your nose and hold for as long as is comfortable before exhaling through your mouth. Let your breathing return to normal.

You find yourself standing in a garden, but not an ordinary garden. This is a garden of two halves. To the left is the summer passed and to the right is the dark of winter still to come, but for now, you walk this middle path between the two. You look left and you can see the summer that has been. It is like looking back on sepia-toned photos, snapshots of instances, good and bad. Of triumphs, failures, and the learning that occurs with each. To the right is the coming winter, the plans that must be made, the excitement of the festivities, and the dark of bleak midwinter.

The left, the past, bright and warm.

The right, the future, dark and cold.

But for now, in this present, you walk between the two. And here in this space you can see and feel the transformative energy that abounds at this time. The annual flowers, the last of their summer colour fading—less vibrant but perhaps more lovely because of it—are beginning to look straggly.

The last of the sunflowers still turn their deep yellow heads towards the fading sun even as their kin wither and die, becoming food for the birds.

The hedgerow is spotted with red. Here the hawthorn forms part of the hedgerow, and the red, red berries are ripe. If you look closer, you'll see the last of the blackberries, still good, but only just. You pluck one from the plant. It bursts as soon as your lips close around it, overripe and warm but deliciously sweet.

All around the garden, you can see the signs of the season. The slowing down. The dying back.

And yet the apple and pear are ripe and juicy. They taste like liquid sunshine.

The hazel tree, too, has much to offer for human and squirrel alike.

A ripening and a dying back, both equal for the moment, but this balance will not last long, and there will be much work to do before the darkness descends. *The harvest must be brought in. You must reap what you have sown, must look back on the lessons learned, and prepare for what may lie ahead. But for now, it is okay to take time and give thanks to this time and the cycles of life and death that have led to this moment and the bounty of the harvest.*

You slip your feet from the confines of their shoes and allow your bare feet to sink into the earth. It is damp and cool. You can feel it between your toes. Feel the energy of the earth, the cooling down, the quieting. This soil, dark and rich, is formed through years of life, death, and decay. It nourishes the trees and plants, which in turn nourish the birds and the beasts, who live, birth, and die themselves, returning back to the land, giving back all they have taken.

This is the energy of this time: balance between the forces of life and death. And as you wander the garden, lose yourself in the delights of the second harvest. This is a busy time, there is much to do, but you also need to take time and enjoy the present.

The autumn equinox gives you time to breathe.

Space to breathe.

When you have rested enough and had your fill of the second harvest, it is time to go back the way you came, for the cycle is not yet finished and there is still work to be done. But you are ready.

Take a deep breath …

And hold it for as long as is comfortable before exhaling. Slowly allow yourself to become aware of your body, the chair or floor where you are sitting or lying, the noises inside the room and the noises outside.

When you are ready, sit up, have a drink of water to aid with the grounding process, and make any notes you feel are important in your journal.

Exercise: Autumn Wreath Making

As with many exercises throughout this book, this one too is aimed at getting out and actively involved with the land where you live. There are many Pagan traditions around the world whereby people bring foliage inside over winter, from the spirit said to reside in the last cutting of corn and fashioned into a dolly to evergreens at the winter solstice. In doing so, those people acted as a protector of the spirit believed to reside in these items, a steward if you will. In such traditions we see the reciprocal nature of spirit work, and so making a wreath using natural items you have found is a good way of carrying on the tradition of bringing nature inside during the darker months. At Mabon, there is so much abundance, and your wreath can be a reflection of this, an act of drawing that abundance into your home and your life.

The first thing you will need to do is—you guessed it—get outside! It doesn't matter if you cannot go far; there will be items you can find in your local landscape, from flowers and foliage to sticks, twigs, and feathers. (When collecting any animal parts, even foraged feathers and bones, do check local laws and bylaws, as these change depending on where you are). Explore those wild places where you live, even if it's only a park or garden. Don't be afraid to root in the earth for stones and empty snail shells. This is one of those exercises where staying clean is frowned upon.

Delight in the search for natural materials. Lose yourself in the moment. Enjoy the feeling of the fresh air on your face and the earth beneath your feet. You might feel self-conscious at first, and that is completely normal. You may get the odd look if there are people around, but that's okay too. Though to be honest, most people will pay you no mind. They are far too busy doing their own thing.

When you get home, it's time to look through your finds. You might decide to discard some items, and if you do, try to make an effort to return them to where you found them. At the very least, put them in the garden. It's about treating these items and what they represent with respect. Spirit still resides in these things, after all. When you are happy with the items you have collected, it is time to gather everything else you will need.

To make your wreath, you will need:

- A wreath base, wire hanger, or vines bound together and shaped as needed
- Craft wire or string (how much will depend on the size of your wreath, but there should be more than enough on a fresh roll)

- Hot glue gun or tacky glue
- Any extra decorations (don't forget, seasonal veg such as squashes can also be used)

When it comes to making your wreath, there are no right or wrong ways of going about it; it's time to let your creative juices flow freely. However, with that said, there is some general guidance you might want to take into consideration. First, start with the base. If you are using wire, then you will need to decide how large your wreath will be, and then you will want to shape it. You may need to double or triple up on the wire thickness if you have lots of decorations, as too flimsy a base will mean your wreath will droop and become misshapen.

If you are using vines or sticks, then you might need to make them supple in order to shape them. To do this, you can soak them in water for at least a few hours if not overnight. When shaping them, use craft wire or string to hold them together. Don't worry if it looks a little messy; you can disguise the string.

Second, as a general rule when decorating your wreath, use the largest items first. Decide on placement and design and have a play around before securing with glue or attaching with wire or string. Next, use the smaller items and smaller still, using these decorations to fill in any gaps. Also, if you are using flowers, odd numbers work better than even according to my florist friend.

And really, that is it. Have fun with the gathering and making of your wreath and hang it on your front door to welcome in the spirit of the season.

Samhain (31st October–1st November)

For many witches, Samhain is the highlight of the wheel. It is the classic season of the witch, and what's not to love? Halloween is the fun, lighthearted side of the holiday, what with candy and sweets, parties and fancy dress. And then we have the serious and spiritual Samhain. For me, it's the best of both worlds: the fun side where we glamorise and make light of those things that frighten us, and the poignant side, the honouring of our beloved dead. We can see this echoed in the season too. There is a beauty in nature at this time, the bright colours contrasted with the darkening days and weather, and there is also an underlying feeling too, the sense that darker times are coming.

At Mabon, it can still feel almost summerlike, but there is no hint of summer at Samhain, at least where I live. Even on those sunny days, there is a bite in the wind and the nights are chill. There is no mistaking that the wheel has turned and the dark half of the year has well and truly arrived.

When I think of Samhain, I have so many memories that are linked to the land, of course many of them associated with Halloween. Trick or treating on the estate with siblings and friends was always a favourite. I can recall even now the smell of the night air, can feel the cold of it mingled with the thrilling pleasure of being out after dark. Oh, how the landscape was transformed! It felt different, wilder. Even as I recall actual Samhain celebrations held out beneath the stars, all of those same feelings are there: the feeling of otherness, of wildness, of the night being alive. The connection to the land and to nature runs through both of these celebrations—the spiritual and the secular.

Of course, to many of us witches, Samhain is quite literally a spiritual experience. If I were a betting woman, I'd wager that at some point or other in your magical journey, you have heard the saying that at this time of year "the veil is thinning." The veil refers to the partition between our earthly, mundane world and the spiritual. How many of us will honour our dead, perhaps hosting a dumb supper or simply making space and time to remember those who came before?

At Samhain, the connection between life and what comes after is very much in the forefront of our minds. At this time of year, we feel the breath of death more keenly, for Samhain is also known as the third harvest, the blood harvest.

Traditionally at this time of year within the cycles of European agriculture, the farmers would cull some of the herd, not only to ensure enough meat to last the leaner and colder months but also as a means of controlling the herd population. Older and weaker animals, those unlikely to last the winter months, would also face being culled so as to make the winter feed go further and last longer. It also served to strengthen the herd for the onset of winter.

Any hunter will tell you that taking the life of an animal, even for food, is no easy thing, and nor should it be. (Perhaps one of the horrors of factory farming is how it has enabled the death of animals on such a scale that it has simply become nothing more than a production line.) So this also adds a layer of sanctity to Samhain. In this way, we see the cycles of life and death at this time of year are closely bound together.

As an animist, the spirits of the land, the dead, and of nature can be felt more keenly at this time. When I talk about spirit work, this is what I mean: a practice that includes all classes of spirit, including the beloved dead and my beloved nature, as well as those spirits of place I have worked to build a connection with. Indeed, oftentimes we can see a crossover in how we work with those spirits; for example, many of us might associate a certain place, tree, or plant with a deceased family member. When my friend's elderly father passed away, she planted a rosebush for him and often spent time talking to him while tending the rosebush. In this example, we can see how the spirits of place, nature spirits, and the spirits of our beloved dead share a connection. All are honoured at this time.

Exercise: Spirit Connection

Samhain is here. It is the dark half of the year, and the veil between the realms is gauzy thin. Continuing to build a connection to the spirits of place, of nature, and, of course, the beloved dead is something that is important at any time but is especially poignant now at Samhain. If you already have a connection, a relationship, then this guided journey can help to strengthen those connections. Don't worry if you are yet to begin cultivating a relationship with your own ancestors or the spirits of land and place, for this journey can be done by beginners and more experienced practitioners alike.

This guided journey aims to help you feel closer and more connected to those spirits with whom you want to build relationships. This includes not only your ancestors but also the spirits of land and nature. It's important to bear in mind that spirit work includes more than just the dead, and this guided journey reinforces that idea.

You can do this journey throughout the days and weeks leading up to and after Samhain. It is particularly helpful to do before ritual or spellwork that involves the spirits, as it can help you get into the right frame of mind.

To begin, then, get into a comfortable position, making sure you are warm enough. As with the other meditations and journeys in this book, you may wish to read through it a few times or record yourself reading it aloud and play it back to yourself. When you are ready, you may start.

Close your eyes.

Just let yourself breathe naturally. Allow your body to relax, to get comfortable and settle down. Notice any itches, tics, or twitches. Let any thoughts come and go, letting them drift on by. Notice how relaxed you feel.

Take a deep breath and hold it for as long as is comfortable before exhaling through your mouth. Again, in through the nose and out through the mouth.

One more time …

You are standing in the street where you live. It's twilight already and the last of the light is fading quickly. The shadows gather and pool. The street is quiet.

You begin walking, any direction; it doesn't matter.

As you walk, notice how cold the evening air is. The bite of winter can be felt in the late autumn wind as it blows leaves from trees and carries them along the pavement and gutter in a frenzied, swirling death dance.

Lose yourself in your surroundings. Notice how the life around you reacts to the changing seasons, to the dark half of the year.

Already the blackbird sings his evening song, a final melancholic call, and in the undergrowth, you can hear a hedgehog snuffle through the fallen leaves and detritus, searching for the final feast before the long slumber of the winter months.

As twilight slips into night, you pass houses with windows that shine soft golden light. As you walk by, you glimpse snapshots of strangers' lives. From the outside looking in, you feel like that invisible other, a part of the Wild Hunt's horde, and can feel the veil between yourself and this other world you have been given a glimpse of.

Soon the streets give way to the softness of earth, to grass and the crunch of fallen leaves beneath your feet, and you find yourself on the edge of a small woods. You are unafraid as you step beneath the boughs.

The scent of decay and rot, not unpleasant but instead rich, almost sweet with a hint of leaf spice, permeates the air. The ground is soft beneath your feet so that it feels like you are standing on a thick carpet that cushions each step.

Death surrounds you here.

You can feel it, touch it, smell it.

As you walk through the woodland, you can feel the spirits all around you. You thought you'd feel alone here in this space, but you don't. Instead, it feels like a homecoming, feels like this place and these spirits have been waiting for you your whole life. They are familiar, leaving you with a sense of déjà vu.

As you walk, listen to what they have to say.

After a while, you don't know how long, you come to a clearing. In the centre is a large, antlered skull. It's full night now and the pale moonlight makes the skull glow, imbuing it with not quite life, but an energy that radiates outwards. You approach and sit on the ground before it.

Is it whispering to you or is it the wind?

The sound rises and swells, and as it does, leaves swirl all around you, tiny whirlwinds that move in time with this haunting melody. You close your eyes, feel your heart beating in your chest, but there's something else too.

Feel the ancestors around you, inside of you. Their blood flows through your veins. You always carry them within you. Just as the forest is alive with death, so too are we. Feel those who came before around you, within you.

Their voices add to the humming of the wind.

Listen to the messages they have for you. Listen to the spirits of the land, of nature, of ancestors, for now is the time of the thinning veil, mirrored by the season, by the sabbat.

When you are ready, allow yourself to become aware of your body, of your breathing. Slowly become aware of sounds inside the room and outside, of the sensations in your body. Slowly stretch your body, your arms, your legs. Wiggle your fingers and toes. When you are ready, open your eyes. Slowly sit up. Have a sip of water to help the grounding process, and make any notes you need to in your journal.

Ritual: Honour and Connection

Even I admit that this next exercise might seem a little cliché. I get it. A cemetery at Samhain hardly seems original, but trust me and you'll see why it's worth it.

The cemetery in my town is quite large and beautiful. I remember being at secondary school (high school for those of you outside of the UK), and our school was right next to the town's cemetery. During those PE lessons when cross-country runs seemed like the worst of all things, some of us would hop over the cemetery wall, hang around for fifteen minutes, and join the middle band of runners on their return. Back then I don't think we really appreciated the quiet beauty of the cemetery. I guess it's the age, the peer pressure of being cool enough or edgy enough or whatever else we were trying to be back in those days. Cemeteries always seem to draw those who are seeking something else, whether that's some quietness, some alone time, or just some youths trying to keep out of sight for ten minutes.

There is a liminal quality to cemeteries that you feel within you. Life and death all in one place. We seem able to recognise it when in places such as this but less so elsewhere, and yet life and death are always within touching distance in nature.

There's also a lot of wildlife in my cemetery, and you may just find there is in yours too. For a start, I don't think I've ever been in a cemetery without trees, usually at least one yew tree. And mature trees are essential in attracting wildlife. They provide shelter, habitats, home, food, fuel, shade, and so much more, supporting a myriad of other creatures. And of course, trees have spirits too.

I guess what I'm saying is that while cemeteries are very much associated with the spirits of the dead, they are also places where spirits of nature and place can be found too. Yes, death does indeed reside here, but so too does life. By making some time to visit your local cemetery, not only can this form a part of your relationship with the land where you live, but it is also a good way of connecting with spirit. It's also a great way of understanding the nuances and energies between different types of spirit.

Before you even get into any of that though, it's important to take into consideration legal and ethical matters. First, the cemetery is a place of rest and respect for those who came before and those who come in remembrance. Any ritual you do will need to take this into account. Also, as with any outdoor ritual, it's worth considering your impact on the environment and any creatures that live in that place.

The aim of this small ritual is to tune in to the rhythms of the land at this place and time, but also to help you see and feel the nuances that can be felt in such places. By doing so, you'll be honing those skills that will allow you to feel such nuances in other places.

The cemetery is a liminal space, and you will need to find the oldest grave within the cemetery. (Check the notice board; there might be information about any groups who look after graves, as they might have some useful information about the history of the cemetery.) This grave can be said to represent the guardian of the cemetery, and so connecting with it can act as a way of gaining a deeper connection that is rooted in the mundane and the spiritual.

For this ritual, you will need:

- ◆ Any white candle in a suitable holder
- ◆ Flowers (or handpicked seasonal foliage)
- ◆ A libation of your choosing (water is perfectly acceptable)

Begin by tidying around the grave, clearing any rubbish and debris. I always find this a meditative act in and of itself. You can sing, chant, or just talk aloud as you go about tidying the area around the grave.

Next, light the candle and place it at the head of the grave, along with the flowers. Hold the libation and say:

Guardian spirit of this liminal space
Where death and life dance in embrace,
Where the realms converge and seep into the land.
I have come to witness, to stop and stand,
To see and feel this moment, this space
Where life and death dance in embrace.
Accept this libation and share with me

Take a sip of the libation before pouring the rest onto the ground next to or on the grave.

The secrets of this place, share with me!

Now, find a comfortable place to sit in silence. Observe the goings-on of the cemetery, people, and animals. Get a feel for the space. Go for a walk. Simply immerse yourself in this space and energy. In doing so, you will begin to get a feel for the different energies that can abound in one space.

Autumn Fun and Magic

Wild food is abundant at this time of year; it is the harvest after all, and wild food is the purest of delights. It's a great feeling: going out, gathering wild food, and making something delicious to share with your loved ones.

Foraging for food really does reinforce the reciprocal nature between us and the spirits of the land, not to mention the land itself. The physical act of interacting with nature, of moving through it in a thoughtful and measured way, such as foraging requires, really does make us focus on our physical selves and the land in a way that we might not otherwise do when just going for a walk.

We must also consider the wider needs of the environment and those other beings who live there. Foraging can be one of those controversial subjects, and whenever I lead foraging walks in my small town, there's always at least one person who accuses me of stealing food from nature. While it is easy to get defensive, it does raise an important question: Is foraging ethical?

The quick answer is yes. There is absolutely a legitimate concern around taking food from the wild, but there are also important considerations that must be taken into account. Foraging should be about taking only what you need for the pot. It isn't about taking everything and hoarding it. If anything, it is in our interest to help maintain healthy habitats and ecosystems so that they are sustainable. In this way, foraging can help bridge the divide we might feel we have with nature.

Another way in which foraging can help link us to the land and to the people who lived there before is by linking these wild foods to folk stories, myth, and legend. For example, it was while researching the elder tree many years ago that I learned about a local piece of folklore whereby the spirit of the elder tree is called "the old woman" and is associated with witches and witchcraft. As you begin to explore both the land and the myths and stories associated with it, you'll begin to gain a deeper insight into the complexity of the relationship between the two.

Exploration: Foraging Locally

Foraging is also a good way of honing your identification skills and learning about what is growing in the local landscape. As always, before taking any wild food home, it's important you are 100 percent sure of what it is and whether or not it is edible. And as a note, just because something is edible, doesn't mean it tastes good! Luckily, wild food that tastes good is bountiful, particularly at this time. A good identification guide and a good plant app, when used in conjunction with one another, can be really beneficial when identifying plants. However, if you are not sure about a plant or fruit, then leave it well alone, even if the doubt is small. Better safe than sorry.

When it comes to safety, you also need to consider clothing and footwear. It's important to dress for the terrain and the weather. If the weather is moderate and the terrain mild, a comfy pair of trainers and some thick trousers such as jeans are adequate. A good pair of walking boots is important when going anywhere wilder than pavement. They are comfy and provide ankle support as well as having good surface grip. And always let someone know where you are going if you are going alone. Apps such as what3words are great if you are going really wild and get into trouble, such as if you get lost or injured. Such apps give your precise location so that you can get the help you need where you need it.

It's also important to consider the laws, including local bylaws, which may contain restrictions in specific places. It's also worth noting that in some places, picking overhanging fruit is illegal without the consent of the owners of the land where the tree is growing. Besides, it's just good manners to ask before picking, and in my own experience, most people are more than willing to share a few of their own fruits.

What to forage? Of course, it will depend on where in the world you are and what grows there, but generally the following foods are ready for picking at this time in my region:

- ◆ Hazelnuts
- ◆ Rowan berries
- ◆ Blackberries

- Apples
- Pears
- Plums
- Rosehips
- Haws (hawthorn berries)
- Sloes

Exercise: Cooking with Foraged Plants

No doubt, this list will look different depending on where you live, but the point is that there is a wide range of foods and drinks that can be made from such foraged finds. Here I will share some of my favourite recipes that require little cooking.

Flavoured Alcohols

These are perhaps the easiest way of using fruits such as blackberries. Some fruits such as sloe are extremely bitter to taste but are fantastic for flavouring alcohol such as gin, vodka, or brandy. To make a flavoured alcohol, simply half fill a jar with your chosen berries and add your chosen alcohol, filling the jar or bottle the rest of the way up. Add a lid and let infuse for at least a month but up to three. Strain into a clean bottle and enjoy. I always give these out as gifts at Yule, and they make a very good offering or libation for wassailing later on in the year. (Wassailing is a type of joyous ritual folk custom whereby songs are sung and alcohol such as cider is poured in orchards or around fruit trees to ensure a bountiful harvest.) I like to take a small amount to my regular foraging place and pour a libation to the land and the spirits as a way of thanking them.

You can even use the alcohol-filled berries in cooking and jam making. A particular favourite of mine is to add the berries to ice cream for a boozy treat.

Pan-Fried Hazelnuts

Though these are delicious fresh from the shell, and though I cannot resist digging into them on the walk home from collecting them, pan-frying these delicious little nuts is my favourite way to have them. Melt a tablespoon of butter in a frying pan over a medium heat and add your shelled nuts. Pan-fry for a few minutes until they begin to turn a light golden colour, and serve warm with a twist of salt and pepper. For nuts with a little more kick, try adding chilli, paprika, and nutmeg to taste. Be warned though, it's better to layer the seasoning, starting with a little. Too much seasoning in cooking is very difficult to remedy! If hazelnuts don't grow where you live, you can make any necessary substitutions using what does grow locally.

Wine-Poached Apples or Pears

Poaching is a cooking method which involves cooking something in gently boiling liquid (like eggs). This recipe is a little more luxurious than poached eggs, though just as simple!

Empty a bottle of wine into a pan along with a cup of sugar and a teaspoon of vanilla essence. Heat gently, stirring constantly until the sugar has dissolved. Add four large pears (or apples) to the mixture, and simmer for around twenty minutes or until the pears are soft. By this time, the wine and sugar elixir should make a lovely syrup in which to serve your deliciously poached fruits.

Discovering More

There are many ways of using up your foraged foods, and there are many books and websites dedicated to such. A quick Google search will return hundreds of hits. And if you are a seasoned cook or simply enjoy experimenting, then why not substitute some ingredients in your favourite recipes with your foraged finds? Wild rocket is a good addition to salad, as is watercress, nasturtium leaves and flowers, and young dandelion greens.

Sunrise and Sunset

At this time of year, especially in the witchcraft world, the focus tends to be on darkness. Halloween and Samhain are easily associated with the dark and death, echoing the themes we can see in the natural world, depending, of course, on where you live. And this is the crux, isn't it? We need to deepen our relationship with the land where we live, so that means getting to know what each season looks and feels like in our own place. In doing so, we can begin to gain a deeper understanding of the wider world. As above, so below, and all that jazz.

With so much emphasis on darkness, it's easy to forget about the light. And I get it; we all do it. I love this time of year for the cosiness of it all. I love nothing more than snuggling in my lamp-and candlelit living room with a blanket about my shoulders, book in hand, and coffee on tap. It always reminds me of being a kid, this darkness. Coming home from school and it being almost dark, steamed kitchen windows from my mum's cooking, and the squeak of the hamster wheel in my bedroom—there are so many memories that flood back. And yet, the growing darkness does indeed contrast against the dwindling light. Because our attention is often taken up with a myriad of other things mundane and magical alike—whether that's work, the school run, Halloween costumes and celebrations, or indeed Samhain rituals—we often miss this nuance. Oh, we notice the big changes all right. How many times do people comment about it getting dark sooner? But we don't really pay much attention to the interplay of light and dark beyond this initial noticing. The fact that so many people do recognise this moment (how many times does it pop up in conversation, again?), if only in passing, makes me think it is an important one.

Exercise: Autumnal Observations

The following exercise is about paying attention to the light and the dark. One of the benefits about this time of year is that the sunrise is later and the sunset earlier, and this makes observing them somewhat easier. Of course, you may well have to balance this against going to and from work, family obligations, and the like, but at least you won't have to wake in the small hours of the morning for the sunrise.

Remember those sun salutations from earlier—the songs of day and night? Well now it's time to return to them. Doing so will allow you to really notice how they have changed as the year has progressed. Though it might be the season of slowing down, and though the sun rises later and sets earlier, we are all too often disconnected from the natural cycles and rhythms. For the vast majority of us, our workaday lives are pretty monotone, even in rewarding careers. I love my day job teaching children and young people with autism. Every day is different. There are always new challenges to work through, fresh opportunities, and yet every day starts and finishes at the same time. So while it might be easier to rise with the sun and observe the sunset because it doesn't involve waking early or staying up late, there will be other barriers that must be overcome. And with a little forward planning, these can be too!

If you can do this every day, then perfect, but if not, aim for at least once or twice a week. It can help to choose the same day every week to help build a habit. By scheduling and setting aside a little time each week, it will make the chances of actually doing it more likely.

Instead of visualising the sunrise and sunset, this time you will be observing them. Again, outside is best, but if for whatever reason it is just not possible, then an open window is perfectly acceptable.

At the sunrise, notice how the light begins to seep into the day. Can you see how it begins to lighten in the east? At first it might appear as a slow brightening and perhaps at other times a splash of light on the horizon. Notice how it spreads. What colours do you see? What about the play of light and dark in the garden or on the street? Notice those places where it seems the shadows stretch and pool for longer. Notice the quality of the light. And at sunset, again pay attention to the sky. Are the moon or stars visible? Are there any stars you notice all the time? For example, does one shine brighter or appear first? What colours do you notice in the sky as it deepens towards blackness?

As well as observing the sunrise and sunset, also take a moment to notice how you feel at these times too. Do these times evoke particular feelings within yourself? Do they bring to mind memories thought long forgotten? Do they inspire?

This activity will allow you to tap into the rhythms of the land where you live at this time of year. It reminds us to slow down and to observe the changes in nature and in ourselves as well, for we, too, are a part of nature.

Autumn's Song

It is these moments, these instances, that can help us connect with the seasons more fully, enriched by our own experiences with land and spirit. Let these moments inspire your own season songs. Here is my season song, an ode to autumn:

The scent of woodsmoke hangs in the damp air,
Mingles with the scent of decay, of wet earth and dying things.
Day is slower to break but all the more glorious for the wait,
Mornings cloaked in swirling mists,
The blackbird's song ethereal, melancholic,
And jewel dewdrops adorn my ebony hair
Like stars arrayed in the darkest depths of the night sky.
Leaves fall to the ground, all reds, oranges, and yellows,
As though the sun has splintered.
They catch on the air and dance their final dance,
Pooling in corners to crunch beneath feet
Or to be thrown in the air with squeals of delight.
Night falls sooner,
Darkness descends
And lays over the quieting land.

Chapter 9
Songs of Winter

◆◆◆◆◆◆

Those first frosted mornings of winter feel like such magic and are the first tangible sign the wheel has moved from one season into the next. Where I live, the ending of autumn and the beginning of winter can often bleed into one another, and so those first frosted mornings are the first tangible signs of winter.

Much like we have seen with the other seasons, winter is a tale of two halves with a sabbat for each. Yule, the winter solstice, is the longest night of the year. It's the traditional festive season with several religions having major festivals or feast days, and that's without even considering New Year's Eve. As such, for many people, the beginning part of winter can feel like a joyous time with a party atmosphere. By the time the wheel rolls around to Imbolc, while enduring the harshest of the winter weather, we're already looking for the return of the growing light, even as snow, ice, and frost still grip the landscape.

I don't do well with the cold. I often joke with my partner it's because I'm tropical. I have Jamaican heritage and yet, all joking aside, there is a beauty to winter that sings to my soul, filling it with joy. It cannot be ignored. Besides, there is no such thing as unsuitable weather, only unsuitable clothing, at least to a point.

There is some element in each of the seasons that draws me in and makes me see the world with beauty, sometimes a much-needed balm for the soul, particularly over the last few years. Winter too is beautiful for sure, but the thing I crave at this time is the solitude the season brings. The quietness. The calm.

My morning coffee in the garden is now in darkness, my dressing gown and slippers swapped for coat and boots. The garden feels different in the cold and dim mornings of winter—no less beautiful than in the summer, just different. The birds are quiet; there's no chatter from the ivy as there is in summer when the sparrows still sleep within. The blackbird is awake though and flies from the ivy to the bare branches of the linden tree, where he sings his melancholic song, a single clear voice, the perfect accompaniment to the cold, dark morning.

Some of my favourite memories of the winter come from when my children were small and amazed at the frost, snow, and ice. The way children explore the world with that sense of wonder and delight is a lesson to us all.

Other blessed times include waiting for the winter sun to rise before taking my dog Boo, the gentlest dog you'd ever meet (it's the wild Patterdale terrier you have to watch for) out for a walk. There's a large playing field a minute or so from my home, and on those mornings when Jack Frost had been there the night before, that field was transformed, all pale skies and white frost and the refracted light of the rising sun as it struck the frost and ice.

The cold beauty. The solitude. The dazzling light and muted mists. The quietness of the land. This is what my soul cries for on mornings such as this, even when I don't realise it. Sometimes, it's not until I'm in the moment that I realise just how much I need it.

Yule (21st–22nd December)

Yule, the winter solstice, has a celebratory air. It marks the longest night and shortest day of the year, the point in the earth's orbit when the sun is at its most southerly point. Yet, it seems to me that long before the wheel turns to this time of year, our minds are already geared towards the festivities of the season. Granted, it isn't normally Yule that steals our attention, but instead Christmas. And it does so simply because of the sheer costs both in terms of money and effort the modern celebration requires.

I worked in retail for many years. It was and still is one of those areas of work that is flexible, making it an obvious choice for parents having to work around childcare arrangements. And let me tell you, as anyone working or who has worked in retail will agree, Christmas starts in the middle of summer! How my colleagues and I would groan as we'd unbox packs of Christmas cards in the middle of July or tinsel in August! And it's not just Christmas either. It seems that the shops are quicker each year to sell their seasonal wares.

What does this have to do with animism and the Wheel of the Year, you may well be thinking. The truth is, this is just one of the tiny, almost imperceptible ways in which we are disconnected from the seasons and the sabbats that mark them. We humans are complex beings, and our understanding of and interaction with the world is made up of many layers. If each one is thrown ever so slightly out of kilter, though each knock may be small, the cumulative effect can be significant.

We also think of Yule, the longest night of the year, as a time of slowing down, of taking our cues from nature, but the reverse is true for us, in this, the Anthropocene. We speed up and rush around preparing for the festive season. Some people might put extra hours in at work to treat their loved ones to something special. For others it's the travel arrangements, finishing work in time to get to where they need to be. Or maybe it's just the extra worry about finances along with the shopping, wrapping, cooking, and, let's not forget, parties.

Whatever the reason, instead of slowing with the land, we do the opposite!

And yet, even in the midst of the rush that is the festive season, there are those moments, instances when we feel the spirit of the season or some feeling deep inside that cannot be easily explained with words.

Christmas Eves in the shop were long shifts, starting earlier and finishing much later than normal, preparing the shop for the sales that start straight after the big day. It was hard work, made harder by the fact that I would have rather been at home with my young children. Most of my colleagues would go to the pub for drinks after, but after the fluorescent lights and constant work of the shop, the busyness of the pub was the last thing I wanted, and so I would say my goodbyes and well-wishes and leave. I'd walk home in the blessed coolness of the night through the empty streets with the darkness wrapped around me. The clear skies with silent stars were a sweet relief.

In those moments, as bone weary as I might have been, as eager to get home to my family as I was, I would take the long way home through a park lined with old trees. I'd walk slowly, trailing my fingers across rough bark, stopping here and there to gaze up at the distant and silent stars through the bare branches, feeling the cold pinch my nose and ears. In those moments, after being so caught up in the world of work and with the pressure of keeping commitments and being there for everyone else, it was a reminder of what was real. It was a moment to just be in that place connected to the earth, the sky, the air.

Yule is also about taking time for ourselves, just as nature retreats into itself. The festivities are great (who doesn't love a good get together with the people we love?), but with everything else going on, it can often be a time when we are facing more pressure than at any other time of year.

The longest night has a peaceful feel to it. In our modern world of twenty-four-hour living and neon-lit cityscapes, we often think of the dark as being a bad thing. We've been raised to fear the dark, to be afraid of what lurks there, for surely it is something sinister, right? But at Yule, the longest night is a time of rest. The dark is not something to be seen as bad or negative, nor as something to be feared. Instead, it should be viewed as akin to the fertile darkness of earth or the dark of the womb: nurturing and safe.

Exercise: Sensory Deprivation

Sensory deprivation is a well-used tool in a number of settings, including in the wellness industry and other areas too. It might sound extreme, but it needn't be so, and is best seen as an umbrella term under which many individual practices reside. In my day job as a teacher working with children with autism, sensory rooms are used to help children and young people regulate their anxieties and emotions. These sensory rooms are darkened rooms with twinkle lights, bubble lamps, and other visual and auditory sensory stimulation tools. Pupils can choose to use whichever they need at that particular time to help induce feelings of calm and relaxation.

With this in mind, then, sensory deprivation—that is, depriving one sense and enhancing the others—is a tool we can use to help evoke particular feelings, sensations, and states of being.

I have already touched on how this time of year can leave us worn out and excited at the same time, which can in turn make us feel out of sync with the land and the spirits that reside there. This exercise aims to redress the balance by allowing us to just be for a moment. It seeks to make use of the darkness of the longest night as a rejuvenator and healer rather than something to be feared, allowing us to take time for ourselves at what can be a busy and stressful time. This exercise is also a good way to begin a shadow work practice. After all, what better time to work with our shadow selves than at the time of the longest night!

Throughout this book, we have sought to connect the sabbats in a meaningful way to the land where we find ourselves. This has involved peeling back the layers of that landscape and indeed our connection to it. Now at Yule, we must take that peeling back of the layers and turn it inwards onto ourselves. It is time to work on ourselves, to peer deep into our own shadows so that we may see how we have changed and will continue to. This is the inner reflection that comes with Yule, the turning inwards towards the self. This exercise is one way we can begin that process.

For this exercise you will need a darkened room, so after nightfall is the most convenient time to do this exercise. The idea is to create your own sensory room, and you can decide what you include. You may wish to have a gentle light source such as a tealight candle in a suitable holder or fairy lights. You might want some white noise such as nature sounds, rain or water sounds, or gentle and relaxing music. Keep a blanket to hand too and make sure you have something comfortable to sit or lie on.

There are other adaptations you can include. For example, if you have a real fear of the dark, then use lamps with low-wattage bulbs to create soft light or add more candles or fairy lights. You can even do this exercise in the daytime with the curtains pulled tight if the idea of doing it at night is just too much. It's important that you reduce any anxiety as much as possible before starting this task, so being comfortable is important.

Once dressed in loose-fitting and comfortable clothes, you are ready to begin. Get into a comfortable position and try some breathing exercises. This might be as simple as noticing each breath, not trying to alter the natural rhythm but just paying attention to the ebb and flow of each breath. You might focus on the movement of your body as you breathe or on the sensations that arise with each breath. You might wish to chant, hum, sing, or simply sit in silence. Whichever you choose is fine, but do stick to one method during each session. So for example, the first time, you might decide to just focus on your breathing, but next time you might want to change things up and try something else. That's absolutely fine and good practice in terms of getting to know what works for you.

The low levels of light, the focus on different senses and sensory perceptions, and the overall feelings of relaxation can allow you to slip easily into a light meditative or trance state. In such a state, you are still fully aware and in control but are more open to information and insight into your own psyche.

When you are ready to end the exercise, do so slowly. Take a deep breath and hold it in for as long as is comfortable before exhaling. As you breathe out, stretch your arms and legs. Repeat this again, shaking out your arms and legs, and once more. When you are ready, turn on the lights and make any notes you need to in your journal. It might be a good idea to repeat this exercise throughout the whole of the Yule period to truly begin to understand yourself and your own dark depths.

Exercise: Yule Decorations

Yule and Christmas are the time of year when many people decorate their homes for the season. If you've been around in the Pagan community for even a very short amount of time, you will have seen there is a lot of crossover between these two celebrations, with similar items, foods, and associations. So much is seasonal, so for me in the UK, this looks like the midwinter greens of ivy, holly, and pine, as well as the red berries of the holly and cotoneaster. And the foods we eat, too, are linked to the Wheel of the Year. The spicy sweetness of preserved summer fruits and vegetables remind us of the summer sun and the energy taken to grow and ripen. The meats from the blood harvest recall the preparation of autumn, as do seasonal vegetables pulled straight from the garden: cabbage, leek, cauliflower, and brussels sprouts. This is what makes Yule special, this interconnectedness of everything; it all comes together at Yule.

But there is another side to this celebration too.

Everything can be bought now, with online shopping meaning even the rarest of items can be obtained with a single click of a button. It is great to have this access and the freedom that comes with it; however, in doing so, we lose something as well. Items once considered extra become just ordinary, the accessible boring. It can also mean there is room for waste, something this time of year is notorious for! In terms of food and drink, it is easy to see where this waste might come from, but more than that, we become distracted with other things, and so what might be obvious can slip through the gaps in our attention, like plastic waste. We all know it is devastating to wildlife, and this time of year is notorious for the stuff, particularly when it comes to buying and disposing of decorations, something that many people do every year. So many of the modern decorations are made from plastics unsuitable for recycling.

This exercise is just one way in which you can get to know the land where you live and what is in season now, and it is also a good way of avoiding plastic waste altogether. As an animist, it's important I consider the impact I have on the land and take measures to reduce that wherever possible. With a little effort, you can decorate your home for Yule using natural items gathered from the local landscape, bringing the spirit of nature indoors to overwinter through the longest night.

You will need to go out to collect items for your decoration, but don't worry, you won't need to go far. Even if you live in more urban areas, there will be things you can collect, such as sprigs of evergreen plants like pine, ivy, and anything that stays green. (If you have pets or children, then make sure you know what it is you are gathering and whether it is safe to have inside.) You can even use herbs such as rosemary, as these are evergreen too. Dried seed heads on long stems in vases make good Yule decorations. The good thing about this activity is that you can unleash your creativity. Think outside the box and really bring the outdoors inside this Yule.

This is one of those exercises that gets you directly involved in the nitty-gritty of working with the genius loci without you realising it. By bringing the outdoors inside, you can tap into the energies of nature more easily.

Imbolc (1st–2nd February)

Imbolc is one of the most overlooked of the sabbats, perhaps owing in part to the fact that it follows two of the most popular and extravagant: Samhain and Yule. It's not just that, however, but depending on where you live in the world, you might also feel a disconnect with how Imbolc is represented. Within lots of Pagan-inspired imagery, particularly online, there are lots of references to spring, and yet where I live, February often brings with it the worst of the winter weather. Snowdrops and dog violets might well flower early in mild conditions, but it's also not surprising when they are covered in snow days or even weeks later.

I also think the other sabbats marked something more tangible. For instance, the solstices marked the longest day and shortest night and vice versa, and the equinoxes marked balance. I wasn't exactly sure what Imbolc was meant to signify, not in a real and meaningful way, at least. I mean, I knew this sabbat marked the midway point between the winter solstice and the spring equinox, Ostara. I had read so countless times. And yet I had no idea what that actually meant in real, practical terms—what it meant in terms of the land and the spirits or what it actually meant to my witchcraft practice.

All of that is without even mentioning that, after the celebrations of Yule, Christmas, and New Year, February can seem a little anticlimactic. There's nothing left to look forward to. We're back into the grind of work after the holidays, the weather is cold, and the summer feels like a long way off. Everything feels, well, a little bit *meh*.

Imbolc, already associated with the returning light, is also associated with candles and coincides with the Christian festival of Candlemas. This link with candles and light is totally relevant for the season.

I remember being in a working group, not quite a coven but more than a circle group. There were four of us altogether, and we'd split the sabbats between us so that we were each responsible for organising two rituals a year. So after picking sabbats from a hat, I was left with Imbolc as one of my two. Just my luck, or so it seemed at the time, for it was the one nobody wanted. I can't remember what I did for that particular Imbolc, only that I must have done something. The fact I can't recall it would seem to signify the moment wasn't that great. Indeed, it was only as l began to consider the Wheel of the Year and the sabbats in an animistic way that I began to feel a deeper connection to Imbolc and what that meant for me and the land where I live.

My morning coffee, taken outside first thing, something that started as a simple act of being present within the land, allowed me to notice the subtle changes of the seasons. It was through this act of being present without attempting to change anything or force interactions that I really began to notice the subtle energies that abound at this time of year. Where once spring had felt so far away, I instead began to notice the subtle differences in the quality of light, the sky at sunrise or sunset. The cool scent of the air, so different from the onset of winter when the sweet, spicy scent of autumnal decay still lingered, is fresh and clean.

Yes, at Imbolc, it is the sky that captures the essence of the season, the hope and promise that comes with knowing the wheel is creaking ever onwards. With it, I began to notice the other subtle signs, such as the small nodules that appeared on the roses in the garden. Sure, a long way off from the promise of spring growth, shiny and green in the way that only spring growth can be, but still, the small green pip-like nodules were indeed a welcome sign.

I think the sky at Imbolc is the most beautiful of the year. I say that while also acknowledging the sky is always beautiful, whether at sunrise or sunset, whether the deep cornflower blue of summer or the dark depths of blackest night. At Imbolc, the beauty of the sky has the power to catch us unaware, perhaps making us gasp with the sheer and unsuspecting beauty of it, alighting on our consciousness as the muse must surely strike for the artist—instantly and fleeting, leaving an imprint on the very soul so strong it cannot be described, only felt.

I like to think such moments strike when we are least expecting them because we need them. Perhaps that's a very human-centric way of looking at it, but it's true, especially if we consider ourselves a part of nature. Sometimes when we have become so distanced from nature, we need to be reminded that it resides within us as much as we within it.

In that moment of witnessing the red sunrise and the pale moonset, it was as though witnessing some great event, the unrolling of a new day even as the night faded. And not in the ordinary way we might think about morning and night, as things that just happen, merely times in the day. Instead as though the unfurling of a flower, an achingly slow moment of luxurious pleasure, a feeling of neither being one thing nor the other but instead holding the promise of everything in between. In that moment was everything that has ever been and everything that is to come balanced against the now.

This dawning of a new day, a moment of such profound beauty, struck me in a moment of profound ordinariness. And when I talk about beauty, I don't just mean the stunning visuals of the two-tone sky and syrupy light that transformed a council estate into a thing of pure beauty, though that was certainly a part of it, I'm sure. Instead, I mean the beauty found in the tranquillity of the moment, the beauty of the ordinary. We so very seldom see this beauty, so blinkered we are as we move through the business and the busyness of the day. At times it can feel as though we are always looking for the extraordinary but in doing so miss the beauty that can be found in the returning light of a simple sunrise at Imbolc.

Ritual: Candle Vigil

In modern Western society, it can seem like the only time we hold vigils is at times of loss or when people come together to take comfort in their hopes for a better future, and yet there is something simple and poignant about holding a vigil to mark the turning of the wheel and truly noticing the incremental changes that occur. This vigil is really about seeing in the sunrise, of making the time to sit and watch as the sky lightens from the east.

To take part in this vigil, you will need:

- White candles, whatever type you have, and suitable holders (You will need at least one candle.)
- A bowl of water

You will need to wake before the sunrise, so you will need to check when that is and set your alarm to wake you before that time. Give yourself enough time to do the things you need to do, such as having a brew and generally just waking up. When you are ready, have a shower or at the very least wash your hands and face.

You may wish to do this exercise outside, and if this is an option, then you really should consider it. The sense of being outside, of feeling the cool air on your face, will help you connect to the moment and to the land. If you cannot do this outside, then sitting by an open window is perfectly acceptable and workable. If you are a part of a group, then this is something that can be done together and can be a nice way to connect as a group.

Set your candles up however you like. If you are using one, then it is enough to place it where you will, with the bowl of water in front of it. If you are using several candles, then you might consider setting a circle and sitting within it.

As the sky begins to brighten at first light, light the candles.

There are no words to say at this vigil, for none are needed. While watching the flickering of the candles and the growing light of dawn, attune to the land around you, this land that has become familiar to you over the course of this book. This vigil is about making space to be alert and present in a very real sense. This simple act of observing in reverence and respect the changes that occur as winter slowly begins to loosen its grasp, that's what's important here: This witnessing of night moving into day at this moment as the wheel turns onwards. This moment as it hovers on the cusp is the energy that abounds at Imbolc. The quiet energy that comes from the land is no longer the restorative rest of Yule but is instead the quiet brewing of anticipation of what might be and the hope and power that is contained in that moment, much like the seed that has overwintered in the cold earth and is now just beginning to respond to the subtle changes that are occurring at the edges.

Simply notice as the sun rises and light fills the morning. When you are ready, pour the water as libation or leave as offering, a drink and bath for the birds perhaps.

If you can do this every morning over the course of a week, even if it is only for ten minutes each day, you will see and notice the difference not only in the land, but within yourself as well. If you cannot do this every day, then make an effort to do it at least once a week throughout February, making any notes in your journal. As you make your notes, consider the way the shift in light patterns makes you feel or how the weather can affect your emotions during this exercise. Do you see this mirrored in the land?

Ritual: Imbolc Divination

The lightening of the sky in the east and the early crocuses and daffodils that might first bloom while frost, snow, and ice still lay over the land are indeed a sure sign that although winter still holds sway, the wheel trundles ever on. This returning light that pierces the gloom of winter, makes it a great time for divination, and this ritual makes use of that traditional association with candles and firelight at this time.

For this ritual, you will need:

- ◆ Four white candles, any type you have on hand with appropriate holders
- ◆ A bowl of water

You can do this divination inside or out, though it will need to be done in darkness so that the water's surface becomes like a mirror. When you have chosen the space, tidy around so it is clean and clear. This act of preparing the space is also a way of preparing ourselves for the task ahead, of clearing and focussing the mind.

Place the bowl in the centre of the prepared space and place the lit candles in a semicircle around one half of the bowl so that you can safely look at the water. Position yourself before the water and dip your finger into the water and dab your closed eyelids, whispering:

Water and light, let me see.
As I will it so shall it be.

Spend a moment or however long is needed in a meditative state. When you are ready, fix your gaze on the surface of the water. Don't try and force anything, but simply notice the reflections. Let each one come and pass, like a thought. Simply acknowledge it and let your mind roam the reflected images. Sometimes information comes as a sense or feeling, sometimes—though very rarely in my own experience—images are clear and the meaning derived straight away. At other times it might be that meaning comes later on or with further exploration while journeying or simply logging your experiences in your journal.

How long the divination lasts depends on many things, including the very mundane issue of pressures on your time. You might get a feeling that it is time to end the session, or perhaps there is a change in atmosphere that signals the end of the divination.

When finished, you can pour the water as an offering to the land and nature and extinguish the candles. Take some time to write down the impressions you had or any thoughts or ideas that came during the divination, even if it's just to get the bare bones down on paper.

Winter Watch

It might just be my own witchcraft understandings and associations at play here, but for me, birds represent the sky, air, and wind. It makes sense, then, to observe them now, at this time when the sky is so ever-changing. Doing so is a way to begin to make your own Imbolc associations more land based and in tune with the nature where you live.

Yes, I mean birdwatching. Don't worry though; you don't need any binoculars, and you don't need to venture far from home. The beauty of this activity is the sheer variety in how it can be performed. You might choose to hang a bird feeder somewhere you can see it from inside and sit and watch what happens. You may wish to sit quietly in your garden and observe the antics of the birds that visit there.

Not only that, but at this time of year, there's plenty of action in the bird world, action that can give important information about the land and the changing seasons. Mild weather at this time can see the early arrival of geese. You might also see some murmurations of the starlings if you are lucky.

In the garden, the birdsong starts earlier so that it is in full swing when I take my morning coffee outside. The real purpose of the dawn chorus is to mark territory and attract mates, and though it won't reach its peak until around March, it is certainly a delight.

By observing the birds, you are also observing other things too, such as the change in the land as the season changes and merges with the next. You'll become aware of fluctuations in weather, light, and the behaviour and actions of other creatures. In noticing such patterns, we can begin to see how the ancients used the natural phenomena to divine meaning from the world around them. We have a tendency to look back in amusement, but perhaps in looking to nature for signs and omens, the ancients understood their relationship with the land around them. As supernatural as these types of divination may indeed sound, really, they are simply knowledge steeped in an understanding of the land. For instance, there will be times you notice the feed lasts longer in the feeders. At first you might worry about a decline in local bird numbers, but it really can be a sign of increased insect activity or the arrival of new plant growth, meaning the birds need to rely less on the food in the feeders.

Bird Folklore

As you begin to get to know and identify the birds that come into your garden or live in your area, finding out about their myths and stories can be a way of further deepening that connection.

The sparrows are a significant feature of my garden, and their activity can shape the feeling of the space. You can hear them in the morning, just as dawn is breaking. It begins with a few cheeps before finally erupting into a full-on chatter, loud in the chill of the late winter morning. They are the first at the birdfeeder and bath. First one, then two, and then three and more, until there are too many to count. They argue among themselves, fighting for a place on the feeder or a turn in the bath. Yes, there is a lot of charm in this common and often overlooked garden bird.

The folklore surrounding them seems to add to this too. For example, their collective nouns include both "a horde" and "a quarrel," both quite apt and show different sides to their group behaviour. There is also a darker side to the symbology of this bird, particularly if one should fly into your home, for it is often said that such an occurrence can signify a death within the household.

Most cultures have folk stories about birds, and by comparing stories from all around the world, you begin to get an idea of just how important these stories are to humanity as a whole. Makes you wonder about that connection again, doesn't it?

Folklore and stories contain the collective knowledge and experience of your ancestors and the people who came before. Within this knowledge are pointers that you can use to help build connection with the land where you live, and in doing so, help you experience it for yourself.

As you begin to identify the birds that visit your garden or live where you do, then the folklore and stories will really begin to take on life. You will build your own associations and connections with the birds you share the land with, which in turn can inform how you will work with them when it comes to working with the spirits of place. This includes animal spirits.

Winter's Song

As the wheel turns and winter deepens before moving towards spring and Ostara, before returning once more to Beltane, you will add your own experiences to the lore that came before.

Winter's breath kisses the air
And leaves in its trail crystalised grass
Like glass.
It crunches underfoot and
Catches the cold light of the winter sun
As it rises,
Setting the world ablaze with fire that burns cold.
An icy wonderland,
The world transformed and oh so still.
Trees bedecked in frosted dew like strings

Of glittering pearls.
Frozen spiderwebs make for good lace
And frost-glazed holly berries for rubies, a blast of colour.
Still.
Everything quiet and still, save the
Plume of my breath, my beating heart
And the
Blackbird as its melodic song
Pierces the morning and sings in
Winter's arrival
Just as it will herald
The departure.

Chapter 10
Spiral Songs

◆◆◆◆◆◆

Here we are almost at the end of this small volume, having traversed the wheel together for one full revolution. You have danced, dipped, and dived through the sabbats that mark the subtle changes of the seasons. You have wandered and roamed and become a wild thing once more.

No doubt you will now be different from when you first set out on this journey, for as the wheel shows us, nature is not static. Everything is in flux. We are a part of nature, ever changing, ever shaped by the land and our perceptions and experiences of it, which in turn shape the land. This is a reciprocal process, this animistic process. The relationship is a symbiotic one.

You have begun on the journey of better understanding the interconnectedness of all things and in doing so have gained a better understanding of the sabbats, and what they mean to you and the land where you live.

You have danced to the melodies of the seasons as the wheel has turned, following the tune as it reaches its crescendo before dipping low to the soothing tones of a lullaby and back again. Other times, it is a hum so low it might not be heard but instead felt, a percussion beat, slow and steady like the pulsing of the earth. You have roamed streets and wooded aisles, a wild thing once more. And so what's next for the intrepid seeker who has glimpsed the secret spirits of the land and is left wanting more? This is the obvious question.

From Ostara, the wheel has trundled on through the sabbats and seasons until we find ourselves back where we started ...

But not quite.

Just as you are not a single entity alone, but are instead an individual part of the whole, constantly changing and growing, so too is the wheel ever turning, one moment shifting into the next so that it becomes difficult to pinpoint that exact moment of becoming. Perhaps you feel this within yourself too. Sometimes these changes happen incrementally so that it seems you don't really notice them at all, and other times it might feel like they come all at once, rushing onwards as the waves rush to the shore. Like the songs of the seasons, the melody changes, speeds up, and slows down, but it never stops.

The wheel trundles ever onwards, each sabbat the same as it was before and yet uniquely different. Yes, the sabbats occur every year and mark the same astrological events they ever have, but each one is new. Every Yule is all the Yule's that came before and yet none of them, just as we are all our ancestors who came before, and yet we are our own individual selves experiencing *this* life for the first time, firsthand. In this way, we can see the wheel isn't really a circle, isn't fixed in place as perhaps we once thought, but instead travels on an endless journey, each sabbat a transient destination.

The wheel isn't a circle. It is a spiral.

Throughout this book, you have worked through exercises all designed to help foster and develop a connection to the land where you find yourself. By connecting the Wheel of the Year to the land and to the cycles and rhythms of that land, you have started that process. In recognising the history of our interactions with the spirit of the land, recorded and encoded in folklore, myth, and tradition, you have taken your place in the never-ending cycle.

That's the hard part, the starting. By now, you'll have the bug, I'm sure. Now that you have worked to build those relationships, the rest is about maintaining them, of keeping up this work already started and growing naturally as a result of your experiences. But fear not, for this is a labour of love, one you will want to keep working at. The songs of the seasons have the alluring call of the siren, and once you've heard that tune, felt it in your bones, you will not be the same again. Instead, you'll spiral and weave your own dance to that music. That's the point, I guess. This is not the end; indeed, there is no end, as our connection to the land where we live and the spirits that reside there is a lifelong connection. But before we part ways, if only for a while, there are a few more points to consider to see you on your way as the next revolution begins…

The Spirit of Inspiration

The season songs are our soundtrack to this wondrous beauty that is life. They inspire us, and this too is a form of spirit—the spirit of inspiration! Okay, so perhaps that isn't what comes to mind when thinking about animism and the Wheel of the Year, but it is important to consider.

The spirit of inspiration is easy to overlook. In this modern age, we seem to have forgotten what it is to feel inspired. We talk about inspirations and aspirations always with a focus on careers or schooling or some other goal focused on capitalist ideas of success, but we never really talk about inspiration in other areas. We never talk about the beauty of a full moon to inspire feelings of magic and wonder within us. (Okay, perhaps we witches do, but you get the point.) This spirit of inspiration creates vital energy. Think about it for just a moment. Without anyone ever having been inspired, where would the world be today? If I were a betting woman, I'd wager we'd be in an even more sorry state than we are now!

The land has always inspired humankind and it's easy to see why, even before you begin to form connections with the spirits of the land. The whole Romantic period in art and poetry focused on those deep internal feelings inspired by nature!

I recently visited the Lake District in Cumbria in the north of England, UK. It's a place of outstanding natural beauty, and I'd wanted to visit ever since I'd been a young girl. One of my favourite authors was Beatrix Potter, my favourite book a big hardback copy of her complete works. Oh, how beautifully illustrated it was! And so it was natural that I should want to visit the place that inspired the stories of Peter Rabbit, Squirrel Nutkin, Mrs. Tiggy-Winkle, and the rest. And I wasn't disappointed either. With mist-shrouded hills, serpentine valleys, and lakes that stretch as far as the eye can see, it's no wonder this place inspired the likes of Wordsworth and Coleridge. And that's without even considering the hidden waterfalls and stone circles!

But it's not just places such as this, as awe inspiring as they are. Inspiration can be found in the small, in the everyday. It can be found in the very landscape you live in, no matter where that is. You don't need to be some great artist to be moved by the beauty of nature, nor do you need to be anywhere extraordinary or exotic.

Allowing the land and nature to move you in this way, being open to the spirit of inspiration, should come easier to you now that you have worked through this book and begun the hard work of making that connection, of laying the foundations of a strong relationship. In fact, if we take a long and honest look at things, you have probably already allowed it in. Have you felt your heart swell at a sight that you might have seen a thousand times before and yet missed completely until that very moment? I know I have. It might be the way the early morning sun catches at the dewdrops that cling to a patch of grass in your garden and how everything sparkles pale golden green. Or how the song of the blackbird on your walk into work brings a little joy to your day. Or maybe it's the stars in the night sky or the sunrise, or a million other things, each a treasure, a marvel rediscovered as though for the first time. What was once boring and overlooked has now been transformed into something else, something more. Or perhaps more accurately, it is us who have been transformed.

You are no longer the same person you once were; none of us are. Instead, you are something else, something more. The veil has slipped and given you a glance of what lies beneath the veneer of ordinariness, a world alive and teeming with spirit. A world where all is connected with threads that are not seen but felt.

How can anything ever be the same again?

This is the spirit of inspiration: that feeling when sitting beneath the cherry blossoms on a warm and sunny spring morning or the first moment of warm sun on your skin after a cold winter. The song of the blackbird as it pierces the perfect silence at sunrise is a personal favourite.

Inspiration energises us. It encourages us to pursue our dreams even when the odds are against us, to create and in turn inspire others. Like the Wheel of the Year, this too is something that never ends, but has a knock-on effect. And so, the next question is, if this spirit of inspiration does indeed create vital energy, what are you doing with yours? What does the spirit of inspiration inspire within you?

Getting Creative

There is no real pressure to feel inspired to do anything, but by now you might feel a bit antsy, like you *want* to do something, commit to something, but perhaps you are just unsure what. The truth is, there are many ways to be inspired and to use those feelings of inspiration to enrich your life and that of your family and friends. It is worth considering how this feeling affects your connection to the land where you live and using it to inspire your practice. Now that you have spent a whole year attuning to the land and nature where you live, you will be able to draw on your experiences and explore them more fully.

This is a good exercise to do especially if you are unsure about the next steps. Letting the spirit of inspiration guide you along with your knowledge, your experience, and the spirits of the land where you live is a great way of really making your practice uniquely your own and deeply meaningful too.

There is often the belief that you have to be good at something in order to do it. I say to hell with that idea! If you enjoy doing something, then you should do it. This is where the spirit of inspiration can guide you to try new things without worrying about whether you are good at them. This is an important part of any practice regardless of the tradition you follow, as you never know what you will discover about yourself. But more than that, it can open up so many doors into your own witchcraft and spirit work practice. It will allow you to engage in different experiences, which in turn can inform your work and your relationship with the spirits that have inspired you. You can use this inspiration in turn to honour those spirits, which in turn strengthens your connections.

See what I mean about circles and spirals?

So now that you have followed the wheel for a year through the cycles that shape the land and the spirits of that land and place, it is time to let your inspiration run wild and see where it will take your relationships to the land and nature.

When it comes to witchcraft generally, there is no one right way, and the same is true when it comes to spirit work, of which working with the genius loci is a part. It's okay if you are unsure what to do next, and part of the journey and growth that comes with witchcraft is working through that. Where do you think grimoires come from? I like to think of them as a witch or magician's own journey of experience, a visual representation of the effect of their own inspired thoughts and the treasured discoveries of that inspiration!

A good next step is to go back to the beginning. Explore some of those concepts you discovered when you first started your own foray into witchcraft. I often think it is good practice to revisit lots of things we encounter in our lives, not just within our witchcraft practices. When you go back and look at those old ideas through the lens of your newly gained experiences and knowledge, you might be surprised to find new insight where once you thought you knew it all before.

Memory and Your Genii Locorum

Time and memory are funny things, aren't they? Tricksy. Sometimes something can feel like it happened only yesterday and a lifetime ago at the same time. Perhaps this is how it feels when you cast your mind back to the start of your journey with your genii locorum? I know it does when I think of my own progression. That journey and all those experiences you have built up with those indwelling spirits of place will have imbued your magic and witchcraft with a deep connection to the land, so much so that your genii locorum can become allies in your work, bringing the vital energies you want to see manifest into other areas of your life.

Crafting a genii locorum spirit bottle is a great way of doing this now that you have worked hard through the course of the year to build a connection to and relationship with the land and the genii locorum. You should also by now have a good familiarity with your local area, and so you might already have a collection of mementos to include in your bottle. These might be special or interesting items gathered on your forays into the wild spaces of your neighbourhood. But first, let's consider what exactly a spirit bottle is and how you can use it in your own practice.

First and foremost, it is important to say a spirit bottle is not a trap and in no way harms or disrespects the spirit. Instead, it acts as an anchor, allowing the spirit to stay in this realm or away from its normal place for longer periods of time. Spirit work requires a lot of energy, both from the practitioner and the spirit itself, and so the spirit bottle or vessel allows the spirit you want to work with to magnify that energy. And because you are using items collected with love and care from the land where you live, it's even more special, almost acting like a signal booster. Those items, whether sticks, stones, feathers, or more, will still retain some essence of the spirit that once inhabited them or from which they came, making them extremely potent when it comes to working with the spirits of the places from which they were gathered. (I must note that different places have different laws with regard to collecting animal parts, even something as innocent as fallen feathers, so be aware when collecting items.)

Having and using a genii locorum spirit bottle means that even on those occasions when you just cannot get out into those special and sacred spaces, you can still work and commune with the spirits of those places. You can give offerings and thanks when it is impossible to get out into the local landscape. You can continue to build your relationship with those spirits in so many ways in your own home.

Exercise: Genii Locorum Spirit Bottle

Making your spirit vessel or bottle needn't cost anything at all and is a great example of how being practical and crafty can add to your witchcraft practice and deepen it. This tool, for that is what a spirit bottle is, is a tool that will help you connect with spirit while also connecting all of those different ideas and beliefs you might hold. For example, being an animist witch who holds the land and the spirits as sacred means that in my mundane life, I try my best to look after those spaces and the wider environment, including recycling and using less plastic, composting, reusing and repurposing items, and all those other things that we tend to think of as "green" in this modern age but were once just a part of everyday living. This spirit bottle seems to encapsulate all of those things, bringing them together to form a whole and embodied practice.

To make your spirit bottle, you will need:

- A clean jar with a lid (I always save food jars and give them a good scrub.)
- Sand (go for play sand so you can be sure it doesn't contain any creatures and is clean)
- Crushed eggshell
- Items from your walks and outings such as stones, feathers, etc.
- White or green candle
- Tweezers

Before you begin crafting your bottle, it's important that you make sure all your natural items are dry, including plants or flowers, else they will begin to go mouldy and rot. To dry any foliage or flowers, you can simply bunch them together and tie with string before hanging for a few days. Alternatively, you can place them in a basket or bowl and place them on a warm windowsill or by a radiator. If you have a dehydrator, you can use that too. When everything is dry, you are ready to begin.

If you want to make your spirit vessel in a ritualised way, then you can by following your normal tradition or practice to set up the space. Otherwise, it is simply enough to light a candle and spend a few moments in quiet meditation bringing to mind your natural space and the feelings inspired when in that place. Welcome the spirits into your crafting area.

Now, when it comes to making any type of spirit vessel, the general idea is to use the smallest items first, so the sand goes in first. Sand is used to represent the land. The very first genii locorum vessel I made, I made the mistake of using soil taken from my area that had small creatures in it, so that endeavour required a trip back out to let them go! Next, I tried compost, but it caused the other items to go mouldy, so sand it is! The point is, trial and error are how we learn, even in witchcraft, so never be afraid to experiment, even if it goes wrong!

Next to go in is the eggshell. This represents the cycle of life, death, and rebirth as well as the transformative processes that occur in nature. Don't be afraid to play around with style. You might want to layer the sand and eggshell to create intricate patterns. Let your own aesthetic tastes take charge!

Once you're happy, the larger items can go in. You might have stones, twigs, and feathers or other items. It's all good! Use the tweezers to arrange the pieces to suit your own tastes. When you are happy with how it looks, it's time to seal the jar using the candle wax to hold the lid in place. The beauty of crafting your own tools is that you can truly make them your own. You might also like to use the same wax to fix stones or other decorations to the lid, but again, let your own tastes and needs dictate.

Now it's time to consecrate your bottle.

Ritual: Spirit Bottle Consecration

Consecrating any ritual tool simply means to dedicate it to its purpose. In the case of your genii locorum spirit bottle, this involves inviting the spirits of the land—represented by the items you have gathered and with perhaps some essence of the spirit still within—to come into the vessel, to make it theirs. This is a simple ritual anyone can do regardless of path or tradition.

For this ritual, you will need:

- Your spirit bottle
- A white or green candle
- A bowl of fresh water

Wash your hands and face before gathering everything you need. Make sacred space if you wish to, however your tradition or practice dictates. This can be as simple as tidying the area, burning cleansing herbs such as sage or rosemary, and washing floors and surfaces with a spiritual water such as Florida water.

Light the candle and spend some time in a meditative state bringing to mind your outdoor spaces, the feelings and atmosphere of those places, the spirits you have built a relationship with. Draw them to you, feel them within your sacred space.

When you are ready, invite them to enter the vessel as and when they will. You can say your own words. They needn't be poetic, and you don't have to recite some long essay, but they should be heartfelt. They should include your intent to work with the spirits and to also honour them.

Feel free to adapt the following passage or use it as a template if you need a little inspiration:

The land that I love, harken to me,
Spirits of the land, wild and free,
Welcome to this sacred space,
Prepared with care, love, and grace,
Come as you will or when I call to you
Into this vessel, fresh and new
Fashioned from items from the land,
And by my own hand,
A vessel, an anchor, a bond between
The mundane, the spiritual, the seen and unseen,

> *Spirits of the land, wild and free,*
> *Spirits of the land, harken to me!*

Allow the candle to burn out if it is a small spell candle. If it is a larger candle and will take too long to burn out, then you can put it out and relight it every time you do work with the genii locorum through the spirit bottle.

Pour the water as an offering to the land either in your garden or in your outdoor space. You can keep the spirit bottle on your altar if you have one. If you don't yet have an altar space or don't have one set up, you can keep it anywhere it will be safe. You can use the spirit bottle whenever you work with the genii locorum or when you want to draw the energies of the land and the spirits to you.

Natural Art

There is something purely magical about the process of creating art, and I'm a big believer in doing things because you enjoy them. Skill or talent is irrelevant when it comes to fun! Or devotion for that matter. Making natural dyes and paints is a good way of bringing elements of nature into your home and using them to decorate items for your altar.

Natural Pigment

There's a reason nature has inspired so many artists—look how beautiful it is! The natural world is indeed ablaze with colour. Take this inspiration a step further by making art with natural pigment. Go out into your local landscape and make a collection of items. This can include soil and earth (you might just be surprised at the range of colours when it comes to earth of different kinds), berries, leaves, and petals. Prep soils and earths by mixing with water. When it comes to berries, extract the juice by pushing them through a sieve and mixing with a little salt and vinegar to help preserve (nobody wants mouldy paint). Petals and leaves are really interesting and are a good way to make prints. This option is perhaps best done in early spring and early summer before everything becomes dry and brittle in summer. Take your flower or leaf and put it between two sheets of paper or between folded fabric such as cotton. With the end of a rolling pin, bash the paper- or fabric-covered leaf. This should extract the pigment, leaving you with leaf and flower prints.

Exercise: Making Berry Ink

Homemade inks are a good way of making the written word even more magical and are a great way of harnessing the power of nature and the land in your spellwork, grimoires, and general magic making. Juicy berries like blackberries are perfect for making inks. They are high in pigment and have a strong colour that will stand out against the page.

To make a simple ink, you will need:

- ♦ 1 cup of berries
- ♦ 1 tbsp salt
- ♦ 1 tbsp vinegar
- ♦ Bowl
- ♦ Spoon
- ♦ Sieve

Begin by pushing the berries through a strainer to extract as much of the juice as possible. Put the juice, salt, and vinegar into a bowl and mix until the salt has dissolved, and that's it! Use your ink to write spells or write in your journal or grimoire.

Ephemeral Art

Perhaps something of a new art form, or rather a new name for something people have always done, ephemeral art is art completely and utterly inspired by nature, created in nature, using only things found in that landscape. Think berries, twigs, stones, shells, leaves, bones, and literally anything in that environment.

While on the surface of it there may seem little point in creating this kind of impermanent art, the truth is there are many benefits! First and foremost, anyone can take part. It doesn't cost any money at all and can be done in any environment—talk about accessibility! Second, it doesn't damage the landscape, though of course, it is up to individuals to ensure they do not disrupt habitats or hurt any creature or being. This includes breaking branches from trees or picking wildflowers. And that's not it either. If you have children and want to incorporate your spirituality into an activity that can be shared with them, this is a fantastic way of doing just that while at the same time instilling in them a respect and love for the natural world.

Any art you create can be dedicated as an offering to the genii locorum or any other spirits you work with, and it develops your own knowledge of the land. You might wish to make a planned ritual of the whole thing or do it whenever the spirit takes you.

Making Ephemeral Art

Begin by thinking about where and when you will make your piece. If you have access to a garden or secure outdoor space, then great stuff. If you are doing it in a public area, there will be some things you might want to take into consideration. The time of day may be important as well as the day itself, especially if you have other constraints on your time such as family commitments, work, or school. You might also need to consider how far you are able or willing to travel to do your art. And that's it!

Now it's time to get out and get creative! Have a look and scour the area for anything you can use in your art, like fallen leaves, pinecones, berries, sticks—whatever you can find. And when you feel you have collected enough, start making. Let your creativity run away with you. Take inspiration from the landscape and from nature; there really is no right or wrong way when it comes to creating art.

When you have finished, dedicate it to the spirits of the land and of nature, and leave it there. The items will disperse naturally, and you'll delight anyone else who happens upon it, in turn hopefully sowing the seeds of connection to land within another. See what I mean about symbiotic relationships and spirals not circles?

Protective Charms

The beautiful thing about witchcraft is that it can connect the seemingly different parts of ourselves and others. While you do not have to be a witch or have a physical practice to build a connection with the spirits of land and place, there is no doubt that for those of us who are witches and do have a practice, then our relationship with our genius loci can strengthen and enhance our crafts. Natural items found out on walks and during our interactions with the land can be used to make protective charms that call on the power of the genius loci to help protect our homes, ourselves, and also the very land itself.

Exercise: Making Protective Charms

There are no right or wrong ways of doing this, and it will very much be informed by the items you have found. Common items handy to have around for making and crafting include:

- String
- Glue
- Craft or garden wire
- Sharp scissors
- Craft knives
- Nails and hammer

♦ General tools

You can use twigs and sticks, plants, flowers, shells…the list goes on. Bind them together using string and glue or gather items in a square of fabric and make a bundle, securing with thread. When you have made your item and are happy with it, hold a simple ritual by lighting a candle and asking the spirit of the land and of those items to protect you or your home from harm. Talk freely and from the heart, letting your relationship and experiences inform your words. Pour water as a libation and leave a suitable offering, such as flowers or native seeds, before putting your charm in a suitable place.

Spiral Song

Through the turning of the wheel and the passing of the seasons, you will be well on your own journey of rediscovery, and oh, what a journey it is! There is much to be found in the familiar, of land and of self, and yet still more to be gleaned as the seasons spiral continuously, the rhythm changing here and there, at times perhaps dangerously so. But the beat is always there, the steady pulse of the land itself.

Winter fades and spring returns,
Melancholy and aching bones give way to hope,
That eternal well that resides in each
And grows until it reaches its peak at the crowning of the sun
On midsummer's day
And ripens on, sweetens with the dog days,
Bursting with golden juice that turns memories rose tinted
As the harvest hangs in the air, and then autumn,
Sepia toned and bittersweet as the gloom deepens towards
The veiled parting.

Aching once more in the desolation of winter,
And yet,
Beating deep within the earth, the hope that will soon spill once more.
And so the spiral continues …

Encore

♦♦♦♦♦♦

Now the time has come for us to part ways once more. It is time to go on, to forge your path armed with the knowledge and understanding of your own experiences and interactions with the land and the spirits.

This is the beauty of the journey; it is never ending. There are always more melodies to discover, more songs to add to this glorious discography of season songs. Indeed, as already discovered, the spiral songs and dances that ebb and flow with the sabbats as the wheel trundles ever onwards...

Farewell for now, my fellow seekers. May we become wild things once more, dancing to the songs of the season and perhaps adding our own melodies to this wondrous symphony that is the interconnectedness of all!

Bibliography

◆◆◆◆◆◆

"A Pleasant Countrey Maying Song," English Broadside Ballad Archive, University of California at Santa Barbara, Department of English, c. 1625, https://ebba.english.ucsb.edu/ballad/20010 /image.

Balfour, M. C. "Legends of the Cars." *Folk-Lore* 2, no. 2 (June 1891): 157–164.

Evans, Arthur J., "The Rollright Stones and Their Folk-Lore," *Folk-Lore* 6 (1895): 5-50.

Hutton, Ronald. *The Stations of the Sun: A History of the Ritual Year in Britain*. Oxford: Oxford University Press, 2011.

Jacobs, Joseph, ed. "The Buried Moon." In *More English Fairy Tales*. London: David Nutt, 1894.

Potter, Beatrix. *Beatrix Potter: The Complete Tales*. The Original and Authorized Edition. New York: Penguin Book, 1997.

Tate, Peter. *Flights of Fancy: Birds in Myth, Legend and Superstition*. London: Arrow Books, 2009.

To Write to the Author

If you wish to contact the author or would like more information about this book, please write to the author in care of Llewellyn Worldwide Ltd. and we will forward your request. Both the author and publisher appreciate hearing from you and learning of your enjoyment of this book and how it has helped you. Llewellyn Worldwide Ltd. cannot guarantee that every letter written to the author can be answered, but all will be forwarded. Please write to:

Emma Kathryn
℅ Llewellyn Worldwide
2143 Wooddale Drive
Woodbury, MN 55125-2989

Please enclose a self-addressed stamped envelope for reply,
or $1.00 to cover costs. If outside the U.S.A., enclose
an international postal reply coupon.

Many of Llewellyn's authors have websites with additional information and resources. For more information, please visit our website at http://www.llewellyn.com.